EASTERN FRONT FROM PRIMARY SOURCES

THE RED ARMY IN COMBAT 1941-1945

EDITED AND INTRODUCED BY BOB CARRUTHERS

Pen & Sword
MILITARY

This edition published in 2013 by
Pen & Sword Military
An imprint of
Pen & Sword Books Ltd
47 Church Street
Barnsley
South Yorkshire
S70 2AS

First published in Great Britain in 2012 in digital format by
Coda Books Ltd.

Copyright © Coda Books Ltd, 2012
Published under licence by Pen & Sword Books Ltd.

ISBN 978 1 78159 135 2

A CIP catalogue record for this book is
available from the British Library

All rights reserved. No part of this book may be reproduced or transmitted in any form or by any means, electronic or mechanical including photocopying, recording or by any information storage and retrieval system, without permission from the Publisher in writing.

Printed and bound by CPI Group (UK) Ltd, Croydon, CR0 4YY

Pen & Sword Books Ltd incorporates the Imprints of Pen & Sword Aviation, Pen & Sword Family History, Pen & Sword Maritime, Pen & Sword Military, Pen & Sword Discovery, Pen & Sword Politics, Pen & Sword Atlas, Pen & Sword Archaeology, Wharncliffe Local History, Wharncliffe True Crime, Wharncliffe Transport, Pen & Sword Select, Pen & Sword Military Classics, Leo Cooper, The Praetorian Press, Claymore Press, Remember When, Seaforth Publishing and Frontline Publishing

For a complete list of Pen & Sword titles please contact
PEN & SWORD BOOKS LIMITED
47 Church Street, Barnsley, South Yorkshire, S70 2AS, England
E-mail: enquiries@pen-and-sword.co.uk
Website: www.pen-and-sword.co.uk

CONTENTS

INTRODUCTION 5
1. RED ARMY GUARDS 8
2. TANKS OF THE RED ARMY 14
3. SOVIET ANTITANK DEFENSE.....................................21
4. NIGHT COMBAT BY RUSSIAN CAVALRY 23
5. SOVIET SADDLE PACKING 26
6. RUSSIAN EMPLOYMENT OF ANTIAIRCRAFT GUNS AGAINST TANKS 32
7. NOTES ON RUSSIAN DEFENSE AGAINST GERMAN TANK ATTACKS 34
8. BREAKTHROUGH AGAINST GERMAN DEFENSES 35
9. RUSSIAN USE OF THE ANTITANK RIFLE.................38
10. RUSSIAN NOTES ON FLANK SECURITY IN A BREAKTHROUGH 39
11. VULNERABLE SPOTS FOR INCENDIARY GRENADES ON GERMAN TANKS 41
12. NIGHT COMBAT BY RUSSIAN CAVALRY.................44
13. TANKS IN NIGHT ACTION 47
14. TRAINING OF RUSSIAN AUTOMATIC RIFLEMEN 50
15. CAVALRY IN MASS 54
16. RUSSIAN ARTILLERY SUPPORT IN TANK ATTACKS 65

17. SOVIET INFILTRATION UNITS IN
    MOUNTAIN WARFARE 69
18. RUSSIAN TANK TACTICS AGAINST
    GERMAN TANKS 74
19. "GERONIMO!" AND THE RED ARMY 77
20. RUSSIAN TANK CAMOUFLAGE IN WINTER 89
21. ON THE WAY! 96
22. RUSSIAN ANTITANK TACTICS 109
23. RUSSIAN EMPLOYMENT OF TANKS 115
24. SOVIET TANKS IN CITY FIGHTING 117
25. RED ARMY OFFICERS' CORPS 123
26. THE RED ARMY INFANTRYMAN 131
    MORE FROM THE SAME SERIES 140

INTRODUCTION

THE HISTORICAL record demonstrates that Adolf Hitler was a gambler who, throughout his notorious career, took a series of calculated risks. Initially these marginal ventures were carefully considered, and Hitler emerged the winner from his high stake bets that Britain and France would remain supine in the face of Hitler's actions in the Rhineland, Sudetenland, Czechoslovakia and Austria. Inevitably Hitler drew the wrong conclusions from his early run of luck and began to make the series of mistakes which were to lead to the outbreak of World War II and his own destruction. The decision to invade Soviet Russia unleashed Hitler's personal nemesis in the form of the Red Army, however, it is arguable that Hitler's biggest mistake of all was to drag a reluctant US into World War II. Even after the Japanese attack on Pearl Harbour Hitler still had the option to keep the US out of the war. In a typical act of self-delusion Hitler, on 11th December 1941, declared war on the largest industrial nation on earth. From that moment onwards the fate of Nazi Germany was sealed. It took some months to awake the sleeping giant, but once the US Juggernaut began to roll the end result of World War II was never in question.

While the US was busy assembling its new armies, navies and air forces, the US Intelligence Service was already beginning to collate intelligence on its new enemy. This information was assembled and disseminated to the troops who needed it, in the form of two main monthly intelligence bulletins. These were Tactical and Technical Trends which first appeared in June 1942 and the Intelligence Bulletin which began to appear from September 1942 onwards.

The main focus for the US was initially on the war with Japan and a great majority of the early reports are concerned with the war in the Pacific. However, as America began to come up to speed US forces were soon engaged in North Africa followed by Sicily, Italy and finally Northern Europe. As the war progressed the requirement for good intelligence of German battlefield tactics became more and more important and in consequence there are more and more reports of German fighting techniques available to us. The vast majority of those reports concerned the fighting in Russia and it is those reports which form the bulk of what you are about to read here.

After the war it soon became apparent that the cold war was already underway and the nature of US intelligence reports quickly changed from a grudgingly pro-soviet stance to guarded watchfulness. The 1946 pieces which are reproduced here were written with a view to facing the Soviets as enemies rather than allies.

The material for the two US intelligence journals was originally collected from British combat reports, German newspapers, captured German documents, German training manuals and various Soviet sources. As such, the quality of much of what was printed was highly variable, some reports are highly accurate while, in others, the precision of the information is questionable to say the least, but that's what makes these reports so fascinating. Regardless of the overall accuracy, this is a priceless glimpse into how the men in the front lines learned about their enemy, and as such it presents us with a invaluable insight into the events of the Eastern Front were perceived at the time when they actually unfolded. The reports also provide us with a host of information concerning the minor aspects of the thousands of tactical combats being waged day in and day out which expand our knowledge of the realities of the fighting in Russia.

Thank you for buying this book. I hope you enjoy reading these long forgotten reports as much as I enjoyed discovering them and collating them for you. Other volumes in this series are already in preparation and I hope you will decide to join me in other discoveries as the series develops.

Bob Carruthers

1. RED ARMY GUARDS

Intelligence Bulletin, March 1946

The awarding of medals and citations for valor and distinguished service figures prominently in boosting Red Army morale. A Soviet soldier whose army work consists chiefly of baking pies in an officers' mess may be the proud wearer of a "Distinguished Cook" badge. Another Red Army G.I. (Krachhoapmeeu) may sport the Red Star, a myriad of campaign ribbons, and a "Distinguished Sniper" badge. Pride of military achievement is inherent among all warriors, and one of the most valued designations a Soviet soldier can earn is to be cited as a "Guardsman." Besides wearing the distinctive Guards badge, the soldier enjoys a great amount of prestige and, moreover, receives double pay.

Guards units are picked Red Army troops who have distinguished themselves by their excellent training, discipline, and courage in battle. The Guards title in the Red Army is significant not only because it was sometimes used during World War II as a means of restoring impaired morale among badly cut up units, but also because the honor combines the traditional Guards of the old Czarist army with the memory of the Soviet Red Guards of 1918.

Under Peter the Great the first Guards regiments (Preobrazhensky and Izmailovsky) were established; others were created in the 18th and 19th centuries. The Czarists Guards were elite units with resplendent uniforms, rigid training, and great traditions. The term "Red Guards" was a designation first applied by Lenin to the groups of armed urban workers who supported the Soviets after the October Revolution. These Red Guards were absorbed into the Red Army early in 1918 and lost their separate identity.

WORLD WAR II REVIVAL

On 18 September 1941, the 100th, 127th, 153d and 161st Rifle Divisions were redesignated 1st through 4th Guards Rifle Divisions. This establishment of Red Army Guards units occurred at a time when the Soviet Government was

These tankers can be spotted as Guardsmen by the Guards badge on their right breasts. Guards units are so designated on their colors and standards. These Red Army men conform to their custom of following the inspecting party with their eyes. They haven't painted Guards badges on the tanks, but many do.

Red Banner awards to units have been important morale raisers. The master sergeant shown here sports a Red Banner award (2d from right). His other morale-raising decorations are (from left): Distinguished Sniper, Red Star (equals a "V" Bronze Star), and Order of Glory 1st Class (equals our DSC).

endeavoring to counteract the effects of initial reverses by associating its defensive war with all the greatest days and traditions of Russia's military past. The war with Germany was termed the Fatherland War; new orders and decorations named for great soldiers of Russia's past were created; and Russian patriotism was drawn upon heavily to furnish the steadfastness and energy necessary to stop and drive back the German invaders.

The awarding of Guards titles in the Red Army is rather elastic. Units from entire armies down to independent battalions can receive the honor. Exceptions to the general rule are the rocket-launcher regiments, all of which have the designation Guards Mortar Regiments as distinguished from ordinary mortar regiments armed with mortars, and the 10 Guards airborne divisions whose employment has been primarily as shock infantry and not as airborne troops.

Red Army pilots raked in the hardware, just like pilots of other forces. This Guardsman has the Red Banner twice, and the Gold Star (top of left breast; the equivalent of the Congressional Medal). On his left pocket is the Order of the British Empire, won protecting Lend-Lease convoys from the Luftwaffe.

Non-Guards units, upon conversion to Guards status, are renumbered in the Guards series; during the war their old numbers were often reassigned to newly activated units. Tank armies, on the other hand, retain their old numbers upon conversion to Guards tank armies.

GUARDS DESIGNATION BOOSTS MORALE

The award of the Guards title to restore impaired morale is reflected in the fact that Guards units, in some cases, did not demonstrate superior fighting ability during the war, and were not specially used as shock troops. However, the Tables of Organization and Equipment of Guards rifle divisions are slightly stronger than those of non-Guards divisions, and officer replacements are assigned to Guards units on a preferential basis.

The great majority of Soviet rifle Divisions to receive the Guards designation were renamed during late 1941, 1942, and early 1943; the last rifle division to become a Guards unit received the title in October 1943. Tank, artillery, and other units continued to be renamed Guards for some months after that. It is believed that no ground units were converted to Guards after early 1944.

About 20 percent of Soviet rifle divisions became Guards units and as many as 30 percent of tank and mechanized units; the title also was liberally awarded to artillery units, air units, and special troops. Almost all of the Red Army's cavalry has been renamed as Guards units.

Individuals assigned to units at the time the units became Guards automatically became Guardsmen and retain the title even if they are later transferred to a non-Guard unit.

Large Guards formations, such as armies, corps and divisions, usually are composed principally of subordinate Guards units.

OTHER MORALE BUILDERS

Contrasting with the Guards title is the designation "shock" which was applied to five armies in 1941 and 1942. These shock armies originally were specially reinforced and their title was a correct description of their intended role. In general they remained active armies, somewhat stronger than average, even after the original distinction of being shock units was lost.

Another morale-building decoration is the "Distinguished" badge. These badges are awarded to all kind of specialists for outstanding work: cooks, snipers, mortar men, scouts, etc.

An important distinction in the Red Army is possession of the Red Banner, which is awarded to units for outstanding bravery and remains perpetually with the unit regardless of changes in the name or number of the organization. Members of Red Banner units are considered under marked obligation to serve with distinction. Should the banner be lost in battle because of faintheartedness, the commander and all officers are subject to court-martial, and the unit is broken up.

In addition, units were renamed after the cities and towns which they liberated; for example, one may meet the Krasnograd 115 Antitank Guards Regiment, which may also be the proud possessor of the Order of the Red Banner.

2. TANKS OF THE RED ARMY

Tactical and Technical Trends, No 5, August 13th 1942

The New Heavy Tank.

Twelve months of war have brought substantial changes in the design of tanks of the Red Army. The new heavy tank has been named the Klementi Voroshilov, commonly referred to as the "KV", is 22 feet long, 10.9 feet wide, 8.9 feet high and weighs 51.2 tons. It has a road-clearance of 1 foot 4 inches, and can ford streams 5-5 1/2 feet deep. Its length permits it to span trenches 12-14 feet wide.

The "KV" is suspended on each side by six slotted wheels which give the outward appearance of double wheels. Each wheel is independently sprung on a rocker arm; the fin of the track is guided through the slot which prevents lateral distortion of the track. There are three return rollers and one idler wheel.

Improvements have been made in the track plate as well as in the method of interlinking them. There are no projections on the outside edges of the track plates on which snow or mud can become firmly lodged. The tread of the track has a grid pattern which insures a firm grip in snow and mud, and reduces sideslipping. Thus snow and mud cleats are not required.

A new method of joining the track plates has been devised. Each section or plate of the track has nine links which are interlocked by a full-floating pin. The pin itself is held in position by small disks or lock washers, these in turn held in place by a spring collar fitting in a recess between each of the nine links of the plate (see sketch). A broken track pin is thus prevented from working out of the links and causing the track to separate and immobilize the tank.

The contoured turret, cast in one piece, weighs approximately

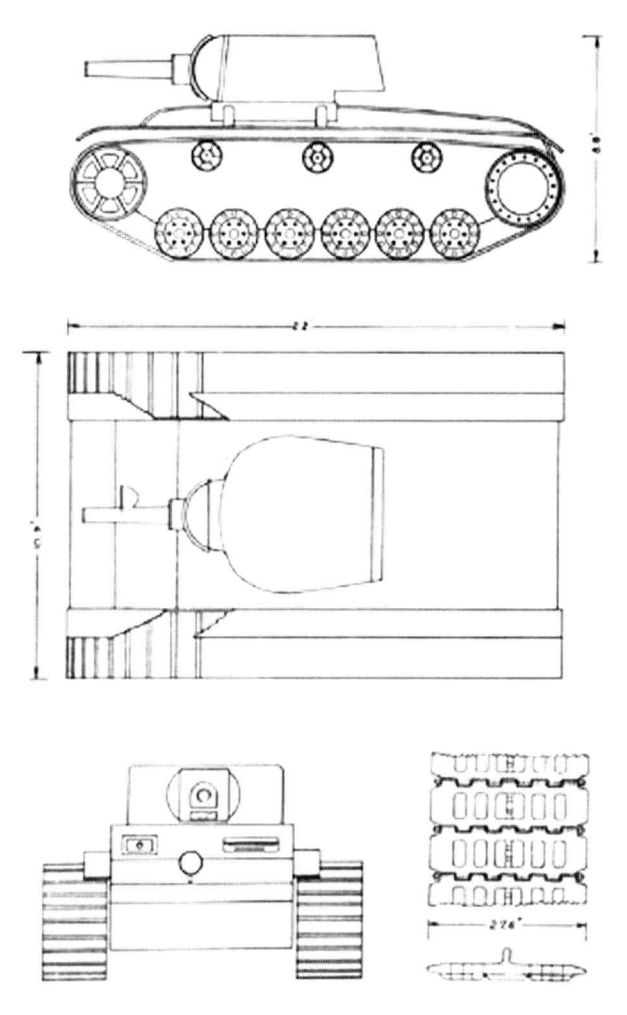

New Russian Heavy Tank (Klementi Voroshilov)

10 tons. The frontal armor of the turret is 3.54 inches thick, making it exceptionally rugged and capable of withstanding sustained enemy fire. It can be revolved 360 degrees either by power or by hand. Heavy steel bars laid on edge are welded at the base of the turret to deflect shells which might cause it to jam.

Following are the data on armament and armor of this tank:
(a) Turret armament:
• 76-mm. long-barrelled gun, (in some models of the KV a 152-

mm. Gun is installed in a specially designed turret).
- One 7.62-mm. MG coaxially mounted with the gun

(b) Hull armament:
- One 7.62-mm. MG forward.
- Two spare 7.62-mm. guns as replacements for the turret or hull guns; or one may be mounted on top of turret for antiaircraft fire, or even used on a tripod for dismounted action.

(c) Armor:
- Front 90 mm. (3.543 inches)
- Sides 75mm (2.952 inches)
- Top 40mm (1.574 inches)
- Engine hatch 30mm (1.181 inches)
- Turret sides 75mm (2.952 inches)
- Rear end 40mm (1.574 inches)
- Under sheathing 30 to 40mm (1.181 to 1.574 inches)

Ninety rounds of AP and incendiary shells are carried for the cannon, the former being stacked behind the loader, the latter being distributed around the turret, under the floor boards, and in the driver's compartment. 3,000 rounds of machine gun ammunition in drums are carried in the turret.

The "KV" is propelled by a 600-horsepower 12-cylinder V-type diesel engine driving through a transmission and final drive to the sprockets at the rear of the tank. The motor is reported to be very noisy. The tank is equipped with both electric and compressed air starters.

It has five forward gears (four regular and one emergency), and one reverse gear. The tank carries 158.5 gallons of fuel inboard and can carry an additional supply in saddle tanks which can be discarded when empty, or prior to going into action. The normal range of action without saddle tanks is 110 to 125 miles across country. A maximum speed of about 21 miles per hour can be attained on an improved road.

The "KV" carries a crew of five consisting of the commander, driver, loader, gunner, and radioman. A mechanic sometimes makes a sixth member of the crew. The posts of the commander, loader, and gunner are in the turret. The driver and radioman ride side by side in a forward position.

The radio is in front on the left of the driver. The antenna is a vertical type mounted forward on the tank. Communication within the tank is by telephone. Inter-tank communication is visual, by either arm-signals or flags.

Tank warfare has taught the Russians lessons which have influenced their tank design. The turret is located well forward to permit tank infantrymen (desyanti, see Tactical and Technical Trends No. 3, page 44) to use it as a shield while riding atop the tank. Every provision has been made to prevent unwelcome riders from getting aboard. There is a lack of external fittings, tools, sharp projections, etc.; this meets the double purpose of eliminating hand grips for enemy hitch-hikers and the chance that a fire bomb or other missile could lodge on the tank. The fender of the tank is very narrow so that "tank hunters" who seek to jump aboard run the risk of being caught in the track. The newer American sponson-type tanks have no fenders as such and have solved these problems largely through basic design. As a further protective measure for the tank crew, the hatch in the top of the turret is so constructed that it cannot be opened from the outside. A special tool is required to open the hatch from the inside.

The Medium Tank - T-34.

High maneuverability and relatively spacious interior arrangement have made this tank a favorite of Soviet tank crews. The Germans themselves have expressed the opinion that the T-34 was the most effective tank they have encountered.

The T-34 is a modified Christie-type tank. It has an overall length of 19 feet 1 inch and is 9 feet 8 inches in width. The low silhouette of the tank (8 feet 6 inches), beside maintaining 1 foot 3 inch road clearance, is an obvious advantage. The tank weighs

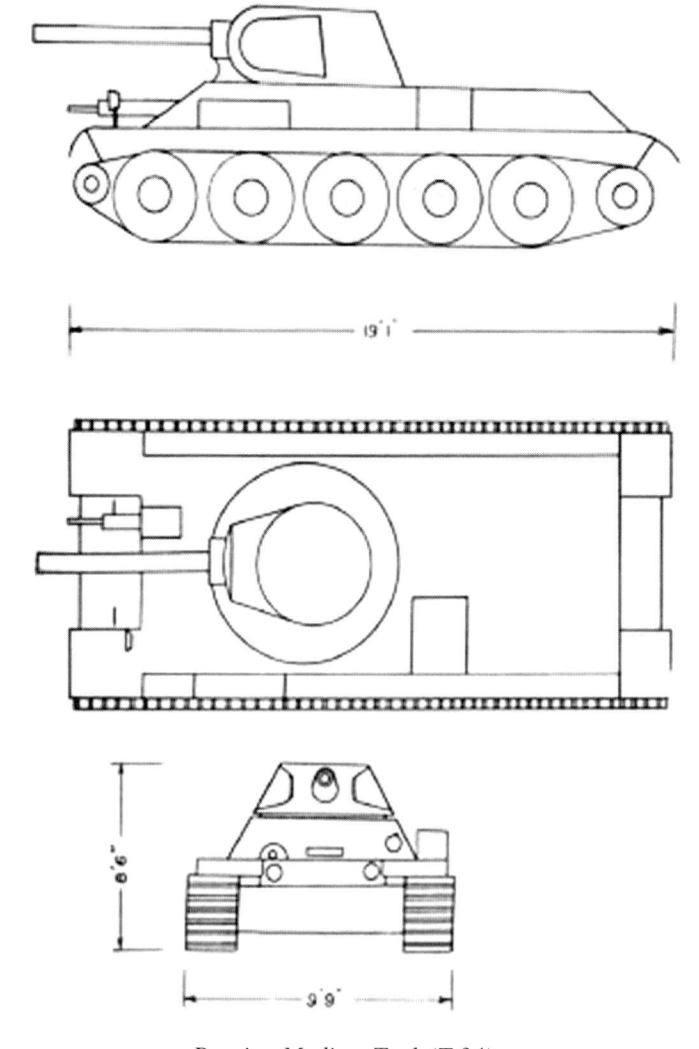

Russian Medium Tank (T-34)

29.7 tons and has a maximum speed of 28-34 miles per hour on roads and 18.5 miles per hour across country. It can surmount the same cross-country obstacles as the "KV" except that its length limits the width of the trenches it can jump to about 11 feet. (See sketch.)

The turret is of the built-up, welded type, equipped with two rotating periscopes mounted on top. Two visors, fitted with bulletproof glass are located on the sides of the turret. The turret may be revolved 360° to permit all-around fire.

The T-34 is powered with a 500-HP diesel motor similar in design to that in the "KV" and can be started either by electricity or compressed air.

The track also is similar to that used on the "KV." It is narrower (21 1/2 inches wide) but has the same design and method of interlinking the plates.

Carrying its normal capacity of 120 gallons of diesel oil, the radius of operation of the T-34 is 150-175 miles. However, this range may be extended by carrying extra fuel tanks strapped to the hull above the fenders.

The tank is manned by a crew of four. The commander, who also acts as loader, and the gunner take stations in the turret. The driver and radio operator are in the forward seats of the hull.

Radio is used only to communicate with higher echelons. Inter-tank communication is by visual signal, while telephone and laryngophones are used between members of the crew.

Following are data on the armament and armor of this tank:

(a) Turret armament:
- One 76-mm. gun (for which 77 rounds of AP and HE shells are carried).
- One 7.62-mm. MG mounted coaxially on the right of the gun.

(b) Hull armament:
- One 7.62-mm. MG in front on the right of the driver (ball mounted).
- One spare 7.62-mm. MG.
- 3,780 rounds of ammunition for the machine guns are carried.

(c) Armor:
- Front 50 mm. (2.00 inches)
- Sides 20 mm (.77 inches)
- Top 20 mm (.77 inches)
- Engine hood 20 mm (.77 inches)
- Turret sides 52 mm (2.04 inches)
- Rear end 45 mm (1.77 inches)

The Light Tank - T-60.

The Soviet Light Tank (T-60) is essentially a gun carrier. It weighs 5.9 tons, carries a crew of two, and is powered with a heavy six-cylinder gasoline engine. It has a radius of action of from 75 to 100 miles and a maximum speed of 24 miles per hour. Its armament includes one 20-mm. automatic cannon and two 7.62-mm. air-cooled machine guns. The armor ranges from .6 to .8 inches in thickness.

The Russian Light Tank - T-26B used as a Flame Thrower.

Many experiments have been conducted by the Red Army to determine the advisability of converting the T-26B (8.4-ton) tank into a flame thrower.

This tank normally carries two 7.62-mm. machine guns, or one 37-mm. anti-tank gun and one 7.62-mm. MG. If the tank is converted to a flame thrower only one machine gun can be carried.

On the experimental model of the T-26B, the (106-gal.) fuel tank for the flame-throwing apparatus was mounted on the tank instead of being towed on a trailer.

Various tests on flame throwers using crude oil (or some similar fuel) show that 10 gallons of fuel per second are consumed under high pressure through a 1.25-inch nozzle, to obtain a range of 100 yards. At this rate, the blast could be expected to last about 10 to 11 seconds. By lessening the pressure, the range is reduced to 25-40 yards and the stream of flame lasts longer.

The question arises whether it is worth-while sacrificing the fire-power of one machine gun for such a short-lived flame.

3. SOVIET ANTITANK DEFENSE

Tactical and Technical Trends, No 12, November 19th 1942

The following observations and sketches on passive Soviet antitank defenses were made by U.S. Military Attaches after a visit to the Gzhatsk-Vyazma front during the latter part of June 1942.

On every possible defensive position the Soviets have constructed barriers, barbed-wire barricades, escarpments, tank traps, and tri-railed cleats. All of these obstacles are supported by fortified dugouts and pillboxes of various sizes, so placed as to cover the approaches of the enemy units, which would be canalized by the barricades.

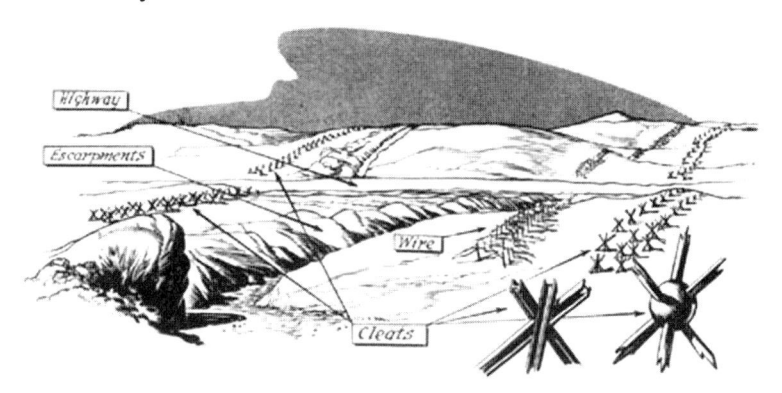

The main antitank escarpment extends perpendicularly from the road, either 200 to 300 yards out, or to a secure flank such as a woods or swamp. The ditch usually follows the contour of the terrain and is normally located on a forward slope so that the rear wall rises far above the front wall. The rear (Soviet) bank of a stream affords an excellent site for an escarpment. Escarpments are dug as nearly level as possible so as to retain water from the snows, rains, or swamps. Dirt excavated from the ditch is thrown to the rear ramp. The escarpment usually is dug about 10 feet deep and about 20 feet wide.

In front of the escarpment is usually placed a barbed-wire barricade of the same length and about 3 feet high and 10 feet wide. This wire is designed principally to keep enemy infantry from utilizing the escarpment as a trench.

The Soviets construct single or multiple rows of tri-railed or 6-inch steel I beams, or 3- to 4-inch pipes welded or bolted together and, depending on the terrain, place them in front or in the rear of escarpments, or sometimes in isolated positions. The advantage of this type of barricade is that it can be prefabricated in the rear and brought up and merely dumped into position.

Rows of posts in checkerboard fashion, 3 feet high and 10 feet wide, strengthen the system. In some areas entire groves of trees were cut down and cleared away, leaving only 3-foot stumps.

Another type of antitank obstacle (shown in sketch below) consisted of parallel ditches about 3 feet deep, 3 feet wide, and 30 feet long, and so spaced as to deny tanks sufficient clearance. Groups of such ditches would be placed at varying angles to neighboring groups, their purpose being to cause tanks to become hung on the edges.

Antitank obstacles and ditches are constructed under the supervision of engineers, but troops of the communication zone and civilians are used to do the digging. There is no special equipment for digging, and it is all by hand.

4. NIGHT COMBAT BY RUSSIAN CAVALRY

Intelligence Bulletin, October 1942

1. GENERAL

The Russians have proved that there is a definite place for horse cavalry in battle, despite the wide use of mechanized forces and airplanes in modern warfare. By operating at night, cavalry avoids attack by aircraft, and moves, dismounts, and strikes with much more surprise than during daylight hours.

2. METHODS OF ATTACK

The success of a night attack depends largely upon careful reconnaissance of the enemy positions. A commander's reconnaissance includes the approaches to the enemy's positions and the location of his firing points and outposts. Before nightfall, all steps have been taken to provide absolute secrecy of movement. The plan of every assault group is worked out in detail. Units are designated to seize outposts and guards, and deal with the automatic riflemen, the machine-gun crews, and the tank crews when they come out of bivouac.

In moving to the point from which the attack is to be made, the Russians do not fire a shot, unless the Germans open fire. In this case all Russian fire power is put into action.

Experience has taught the Russians that it is difficult for cavalry to use artillery in night operations, except while on the defensive. Normally, the cavalry regiments and squadrons take along their heavy machine guns in carts. The machine guns are capable of accomplishing the mission usually assigned to artillery. Antitank units are equipped with antitank weapons, grenades, and bottles of gasoline ("Molotov cocktails").

All equipment is carefully inspected before the cavalry leaves for the attack. Stirrups are wrapped with felt or straw. At a point about 3 to 5 miles from the enemy positions, the machine-gun carts are left in he open and the guns and mortars are carried in pack. The troops dismount again in open areas near the enemy outposts, and the horse-holders hide the horses.

If the mission is to seize a particular point, machine guns and mortars support the action without a let-up until the point is taken. If the mission is to destroy an enemy unit, the troops return when the mission has been accomplished. In this case the machine guns and mortars are placed in positions where they can also provide fire for the withdrawal of the units, in addition to supporting the attack.

These night attacks are planned so as to be completed 2 or 3 hours before daybreak. The Russians need this time interval in order to return to their original positions without being exposed to air attacks.

3. EXAMPLE OF TYPICAL ATTACK

The following is quoted from a Russian report as an example of typical cavalry night operations against a village:

"Two days were required to prepare this attack. The village was 22 kilometers (about 14 miles) from our division position. A troop had been sent out on reconnaissance. It went out on the highway, concealed itself in the forest, and observed road movements; it determined the enemy strength, location of outposts, and location both of tank parks and night bivouacs, as well as the headquarters and rear elements.

"The approaches to the town were important. West and south were two ravines too rough for tanks. The decision was to attack from the north and east. These directions would permit cutting off any attempt of the Germans to withdraw along the highway which ran north of the city. They would catch the enemy under crossfires and at the same time avoid danger of firing on our own troops. Since one regiment attacked from north and the other from east to west, this danger was averted.

"The division moved out in two columns at 1900; at 2400 it assembled 3 kilometers (about 2 miles) from the town, dismounted at once; and went into action. To insure surprise, the attack was made without the use of signals. The outguards were jumped without noise, and the units advanced on the bridge in the town. Here three German guards opened fire, but it was too late. Our troops threw grenades into the houses used as quarters, the assault groups attacked the firing positions, and 15 tanks were put out of action. The remaining tanks moved to the highway, but our engineer units had blown up the bridge. The fight ended at 0500, and from then until daylight (in December, about 0800) the troops returned to their position unnoticed by enemy aircraft.

"Our missions are usually for the purpose of opening the way for the infantry.

"As a result of these attacks, the Germans are now posting strong outguards, and even more careful reconnaissance is required.

"During such night attacks the Germans try to capture our horse-holders."

5. SOVIET SADDLE PACKING

Tactical and Technical Trends, No 42, January 13th 1944

Horse cavalry has definite advantages of silence and ability to negotiate wooded country where tank travel would be extremely difficult. The Russians are reported to have equipped their cavalry with antitank weapons, and used mounted men in coordination with tanks and airplanes in a new and distinctive type of action.

The following description of the packing of the "PTRD" Protivo-Tankovoye Ruzhyo Degtyarev (Degtyarev* antitank rifle), a remarkably long-barreled, single shot, bolt-action shoulder weapon, carried on a pack saddle or ordinary cavalry saddle, was taken from an official Soviet source.

a. Transportation on a Cavalry-Type Riding Saddle (figure 1)

(1) Necessary Parts

For carrying an antitank rifle, the following pack equipment is used:

(a) Metal device for mounting the AT rifle - 1 set
(b) Saddle bags - 2 pairs
(c) Breastband with neck pad - 1 set
(d) Breeching with tail strap - 1 set
(e) Saddle-girth (an additional belly-band) - 1
(f) Feed bag - 1
(g) Wooden boxes for the ammunition - 4

(2) Description

(a) The metal pack device (below) consists of a beam (1) with five holes to receive the U-clamps and the brackets

---

*[Soviet ordnance engineer - and designer of machine guns]

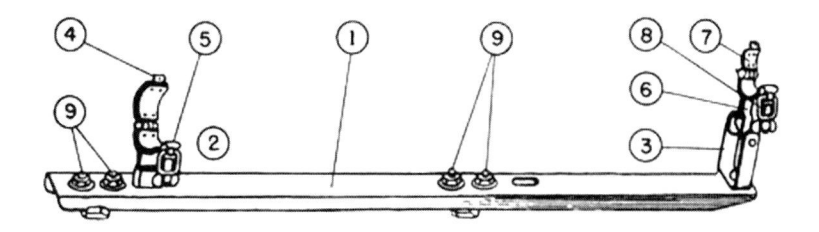

(supports) — one fixed (2) and one movable (3). The fixed bracket is welded to the beam, and the movable bracket is fastened to the beam with a bolt. The fixed bracket has a top strap (4) and a lock (5) which are hinged. The movable bracket has a revolving yoke (6) with a hinged fastening strap (7) and lock (8). Two U-clamps with nuts and washers (9) hold the metal device to the saddle bows.

(b) The saddle bags carry the boxes with 120 rounds of ammunition.

(c) The breastband and the breeching with tail strap keep the saddle with its packed load from slipping forward and backward with a change of pace or in going over rough country.

(d) The saddle-girth (an additional belly-band) strengthens the whole pack arrangement, including the feed bag and spare parts and appurtenances.

(e) The feed bag holds the things necessary for the horse's care, the spare parts and the equipment belonging to the AT rifle.

(f) The wooden boxes carry the ammunition. The shape and dimensions of the boxes correspond to the inside dimensions of the saddle bags.

(3) Assembly

The assembly of the riding saddle is carried out according to the following directions. It is recommended that a second saddle cloth be put underneath for greater softness.

(a) The breastband and breeching are fastened on by means of connecting straps to the breeching and breastband rings of the saddle cloth cover on the right side.

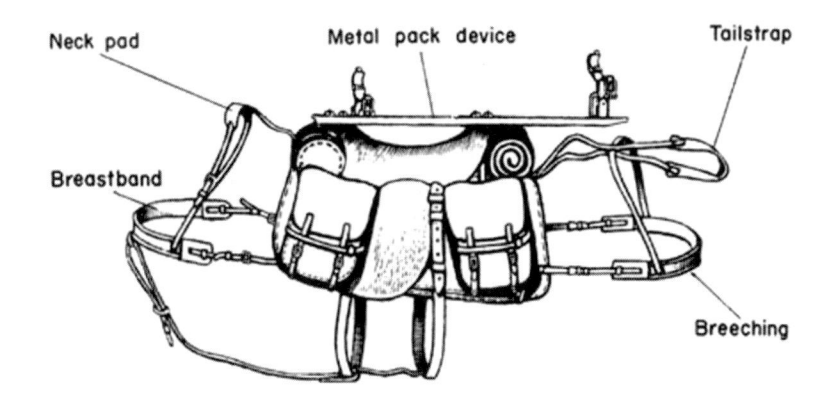

Neck pad — Metal pack device — Tailstrap — Breastband — Breeching

(b) The breastband and breeching are next fastened onto the left side at the time of saddling and adjusting.

(c) The breastband is then connected to the front saddle bow by the neckpad straps.

(d) The breeching is finally connected to the rear saddle bow and the tail strap by two straps fastened onto the bow and tail strap.

(e) The saddle bags are put on the saddle bows in the usual manner.

(f) The metal pack device is fastened to the saddle bows by two U-clamps. For this the U-clamps are passed underneath the saddle bows so that they encircle them and project across the clamps.

(g) The beam is placed fixed bracket forward with its holes over the U-clamp bolts and is fastened down with washers and nuts tightened as far as possible.

(4) Method of Packing

The saddle as it is assembled is packed as follows (figure 1).

(a) The wooden boxes with the shells are put into the saddle bags and fastened with pack straps.

(b) Saddle pockets with oats are packed on top of the front saddle bags and fastened with pack straps.

(c) The feed bag with the articles necessary for the horse's care, and the spare parts and equipment for the AT rifle are placed in the middle, across the saddle, and fastened down with the saddle by the saddle girth.

(d) The AT rifle is then put into the bracket yokes, breech forward, muzzle to the rear. The gun is placed so that the sight is up and the back plate in a horizontal position; the mounting collar of the rifle must be even with the edges of the yoke of the rear bracket. The rifle is fastened to the device by means of the top straps and locks of the yokes. If the horse's neck permits, the gun may be fastened from four to six inches forward of the normal position. Unpacking is done in an order reverse to that of packing.

(5) Method of Firing From the Horse

When it is necessary to fire from the horse, the gun is removed only from the yoke of the front fixed bracket, remaining fastened by the rear swivel yoke. It is possible to fire at aerial targets up to an angle of 70 degrees in any direction (figure 2). In firing from the horse at targets on the ground (figure 3), the horse must stand 18 inches to two feet lower than the level of the gunner. To accomplish this, a pit, trench, or any kind of irregularity of terrain must be used. Stumps, fallen timber or rocks, can be used

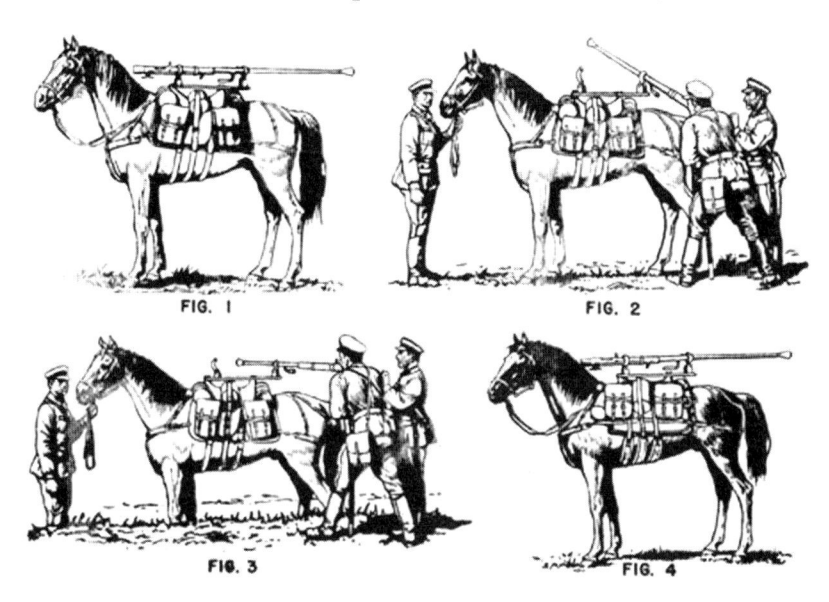

FIG. 1

FIG. 2

FIG. 3

FIG. 4

successfully. If there is no natural elevation a soldier lying on the ground may be used to stand upon.

Transportation on a Pack Saddle, 1937 Model

This saddle (figure 4) has the same appearance as the riding saddle. However, the sketch has been carefully checked and is believed to be correct.

If the unit has a pack saddle, model 1937, it can be suitably used for transporting an AT rifle with the addition of two pairs of saddle bags and the metal device. The ammunition may be carried on a pack saddle, model 1937, in one of the following ways:

(1) In the two pairs of saddle bags, as on the cavalry type riding saddle (figure 1).

(2) On a hanging metal frame, on which the ammunition boxes are placed and fastened with rope (not shown as packed on horse).

(3) In hanging cases or ammunition boxes, into which the shells are put.

The pack saddle is assembled in the usual manner. The

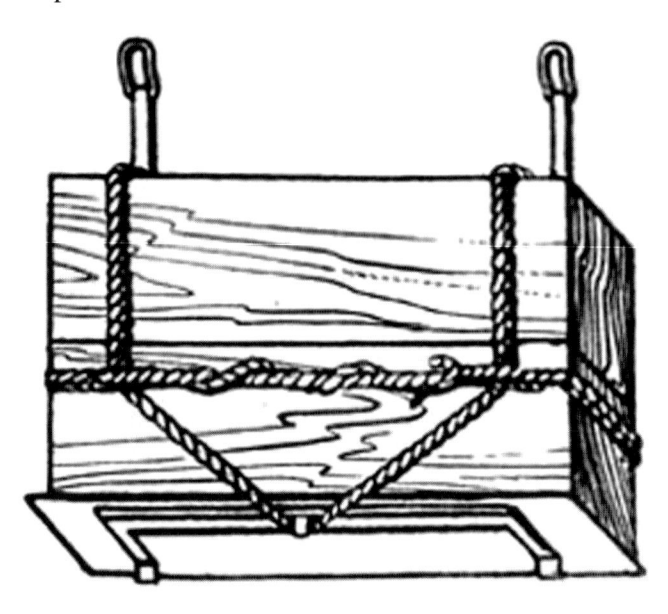

fastening of the metal pack equipment and likewise the manner of packing in carrying shells is the same as for the cavalry type riding saddle (figure 1). When hanging frames are used for carrying the boxes it is necessary to have wooden platforms on the reversible frames, made to the size of the frames, to which ammunition boxes are fastened with ropes. The military unit must itself procure the wooden platforms. The suspended frames and cases are hung from hooks of the saddle bows and secured to the horse with the additional belly-band which goes with the pack saddle.

6. RUSSIAN EMPLOYMENT OF ANTIAIRCRAFT GUNS AGAINST TANKS

Tactical and Technical Trends, No 7, September 10th 1942

Like the Germans, the Russians have found that it is profitable to allot antiaircraft guns a secondary mission of antitank defense. The following comments on antitank employment of these guns are taken from a recent issue of the semiofficial "Red Star".

"In the Russo-German War the Red Army antiaircraft artillery has learned to combat tanks as well as planes. Dual-purpose antiaircraft guns make good antitank guns because of their high muzzle velocity, high rate of fire, and 360° traverse.

"In the first 6 months of the war, Red Army antiaircraft artillery fired in self-defense at enemy tanks which broke through to the battery positions. Gradually, however, the antiaircraft artillery became an organic part of the antitank defensive system. In numerous instances, Russian antiaircraft guns have successfully repulsed attacks of large tank units.

"The antiaircraft units learned that most tactical operations seem to divide themselves into two phases. In the first phase, Russian army artillery concentrates heavy fire on enemy tanks before they can jump off. It then lays down a screen of fire to prevent the enemy tanks from approaching the Russian forward line of defense and breaking up infantry formations. In this stage the antiaircraft units are busily engaged in repelling the attacks of enemy aircraft, particularly dive bombers, which attempt to open the way for the tanks.

"In the second phase, after German tanks have broken into the initial line of defense, or deeper, the German aviation generally shifts its attention to Russian units reserved for counterattack. In this comparative lull, antiaircraft guns fire at the German tanks by direct laying; the shorter the range, the more effective the fire.

"It must always be remembered, however, that the first mission of antiaircraft artillery is defense against planes. In areas where there is insufficient antitank artillery, antiaircraft guns must be employed to drive off tanks which approach the battery positions or threaten to break up the battle formations of Russian troops.

"In order to combat enemy mechanized forces successfully, the antiaircraft artillery must prepare its antitank defense in advance. When the guns go into position they must be ready to open fire against attacking tanks immediately. To establish such a system it is necessary to:

1) Make a complete study of the surrounding terrain, with particular regard to possible tank approaches;
2) Determine the sector of fire for each gun, including ranges to key reference points;
3) Build the minimum amount of field fortifications necessary;
4) Establish special antitank observation points.

"All antiaircraft personnel not working at the guns during a tank attack take up positions in the vicinity and use hand grenades, gasoline bottles, or small-arms armor-piercing bullets against the enemy tanks."

7. NOTES ON RUSSIAN DEFENSE AGAINST GERMAN TANK ATTACKS

Tactical and Technical Trends, No 9, October 8th 1942

The following notes on Russian methods of defense against a tank attack are taken from an article which appeared recently in the Soviet press.

German tank attacks generally follow the main road in the direction of the axis of the Russian communication lines. The attack opens with the shelling of the main road, thus covering the infiltration of small groups of automatic riflemen, who attempt to destroy the Soviet gun crews. Then three or four German tanks appear at a distance of a half mile or more, and open random fire to draw and locate the opposing antitank guns.

If the artillery defense is well organized, "the German tank attack invariably ends in failure." Long-range artillery has the mission of destroying the enemy tanks in assembly areas and in defiles prior to the attack. After the tanks have crossed their line of departure and broken through the forward positions, the antitank system comes into operation.

Antitank-gun crews operate on the principle of direct fire. Crews are taught not to fire at tanks at random, but to carefully pick and choose the most vulnerable spots; for example, the sides. Hits on the turret generally ricochet and even a direct hit on the turret will not necessarily destroy the tank's crew; the tank can still run and continue to fire with its remaining machine guns. Where the tracks are damaged, however, the tank is stopped and presents a very easy target.

8. BREAKTHROUGH AGAINST GERMAN DEFENSES

Tactical and Technical Trends, No 10, October 22nd 1942

The German defensive system employed on one sector of the Eastern Front and the methods employed by Soviet infantry and artillery units in breaking through these defenses are described in the following article written by a Red Army officer:

"In many battles on the Leningrad front, it has been ascertained that the German system of defense is usually based on the establishment of a series of separate firing points which mutually support each other. In one small operation, the distinguishing characteristics of their defenses were irregularity of pattern, and the width of front covered in establishing these firing points. They were placed along two general lines. Some had embrasures and overhead cover while others were open. At distances from 50 to 200 yards in the rear were dugouts used for rest purposes, or for protection from artillery and machine-gun fire.

"In the forward firing points were the German light and heavy machine guns. Some of these were protected by a single row of barbed wire. In the rear firing points were mortars and light artillery. All firing points were assigned regular and supplementary sectors of fire. The sectors were overlapping and, in the case of machine guns, final protective lines were interlocking. Initial fire adjustment was made on the east bank of the river, the Soviet jump-off line. Mortar fire was used en masse and was shifted from target to target. In their retreat the Germans had burned all villages on the east bank of the river, thus materially improving their observation and field of fire.

"After careful study of the terrain and the enemy defenses,

the Red Army regimental commander decided to strike at the enemy center of resistance near the church. After it had been reduced, it would then be possible to make a flank attack to the north, or to strike at the village held by the 6th Company of the German infantry. The local defenses of the latter comprised only four completed firing points, which were occupied by two light and two heavy machine guns. Two of the emplacements were of the open type, and communication between them and to the rear was difficult because of the heavy brush.

"On the morning of the attack, the Red Army infantry was deployed along the east bank of the river. After the artillery preparation, during which the Germans followed their customary practice of taking cover in their dugouts on the rear slopes, the infantry jumped off at dawn. As the artillery fire was lifted to the rear firing points and enemy reserve concentrations, our mortars and machine guns placed direct fire on the forward firing points. The result was that the Germans were so pinned down that they were unable to get back to their firing positions. Our small-arms weapons which were brought forward proceeded to destroy the effectiveness of the forward firing points by direct fire at the embrasures. Meanwhile, the artillery and mortars kept up neutralizing fire on the rear firing points.

"Attacking in formation of two battalions in line, one in reserve, our leading company was able to capture the enemy positions near the church. It was then possible for the remainder of the two attacking battalions, with supporting artillery and machine-gun fire, to develop their attack to the north and to southwest. By committing his reserve battalion at the proper time, the Red Army commander succeeded in occupying all three villages by noon.

"Several important conclusions may be drawn from the above tactical operation. First of all, it is necessary to utilize every means of reconnaissance to discover as nearly as possible the exact positions of the enemy's forward firing points and his main line of resistance. A plan for coordinated infantry-artillery action must then be drawn up. In this plan it is essential to designate which unit will dispose of each individual firing point, and when and how it will be done. Reserve units must be designated to deal with new firing points as they are discovered.

"Fire and movement are still the cardinal principles of infantry, down to the last rifleman. They must eliminate enemy riflemen, machine-gun nests, etc. as they move forward across the battlefield. They must use every means to discover and destroy the enemy before he can employ direct fire.

"The artillery is not the only arm which can neutralize a firing point. Infantry with light mortar, machine-gun, and automatic rifle fire can also be used to this end, especially in cases where the enemy's cover is light or non-existent. It is necessary to have good observation of the field of fire for our infantry and to deny the same to the enemy. If these precepts are followed, fire superiority and the success of the attack will be assured."

9. RUSSIAN USE OF THE ANTITANK RIFLE

Intelligence Bulletin, November 1942

In destroying German tanks, Russian antitank riflemen follow a set of directions, which are given here in condensed form as a matter of information:

"1. Show daring. Let the enemy tanks come within 200 yards or closer. The best range is 100 to 200 yards. Don't let the enemy fire lead you to open your own fire too soon.

"2. The antitank rifle can fire 8 to 10 rounds per minute, if the gunner and his assistant use teamwork. The gunner opens and closes the breech, aims, and fires; the assistant, lying on his right, cleans and oils the shell and places it in the chamber.

"3. Remember that for a distance of as much as 400 yards, the effect of the wind need not be considered.

"4. Remember the deflection correction for the movement of the tank. At a speed of 22.5 miles per hour, a lead of 1 yard is required for every 100 yards of range.

"5. Aim for the rear of the turret—the gunner and ammunition are there. If you hit the ammunition, you can blow up the tank.

"6. Fire at the center of the rear half of the tank—the motor and the fuel containers are there. If you hit either one, you will put the tank out of action.

"7. A well-camouflaged gun crew can put any tank out of action with well-aimed shots, and can block a road to a whole column of tanks."

10. RUSSIAN NOTES ON FLANK SECURITY IN A BREAKTHROUGH

Tactical and Technical Trends, No 28, July 1st 1943

The following is extracted from an article written by two Russian Colonels and published in the Soviet Army newspaper, Red Star.

a. General

In a modern military operation the flanks play a decisive role because of their vulnerability. In any type of battle, success will in a large measure depend on the action on the flanks. In the attack, the principal stress in much of present-day fighting is laid on widening of the flanks and consolidating the corridor created by the breakthrough of enemy positions. In the defense every effort is bent toward holding the positions on the flanks of the hostile breakthrough and cutting the enemy wedge by counterattacking.

b. Consolidation of Flanks

In choosing the direction for a breakthrough, it is unwise to leave enemy strongpoints on the flanks. It is necessary, however, to consolidate the flanks and widen them with all means available simultaneously with the advance. Experience has proven that the Germans launch their counterattacks primarily against the flanks. Rapid maneuver of reserves is the basis of German defensive tactics. Therefore, maximum flank security must be the prime consideration. Units must be designated to consolidate the flank terrain and widen the sector of breakthrough immediately after spearheads have been driven into the enemy lines.

It is not sufficient for flank security to use large numbers of troops only. These flank troops must have a maximum of equipment and be able to throw up strong field fortifications in case of change-over to defense. under heavy enemy pressure. It is most important to hold the flanks until breakthrough units wipe out the whole system of the enemy defense. Wide use must be made of all types of obstacles, including minefields, on the flanks.

c. Ratio of Width of Breakthrough to Depth

It has been established that the desirable ratio between the width and depth of the sector of breakthrough is approximately 1 to 2. For instance, if the width of the breakthrough is 4 miles, the depth should not exceed from 8 to 9 miles. If the units brought into the breach encounter fresh, strong reserves in the depth of the enemy positions, it is necessary to throw in new forces, an operation possible only when the gap is sufficiently wide.

11. VULNERABLE SPOTS FOR INCENDIARY GRENADES ON GERMAN TANKS

Tactical and Technical Trends, No 22, April 8th 1943

In attacking enemy tanks at close quarters with Molotov cocktails or incendiaries, the air intakes are among the most vulnerable points. It is important, therefore, that the location of these intakes and outlets be known, as the flame and fumes of a grenade thrown against an intake while the engine is running will be sucked inside, but if the grenade lands on an outlet, they will be blown clear of the tank.

The best targets are the flat top-plates behind the turret. Side intakes are invariably protected by a vertical baffle. The accompanying sketches show the "soft spots" in German tanks Pz.Kw. 2, 3, and 4.

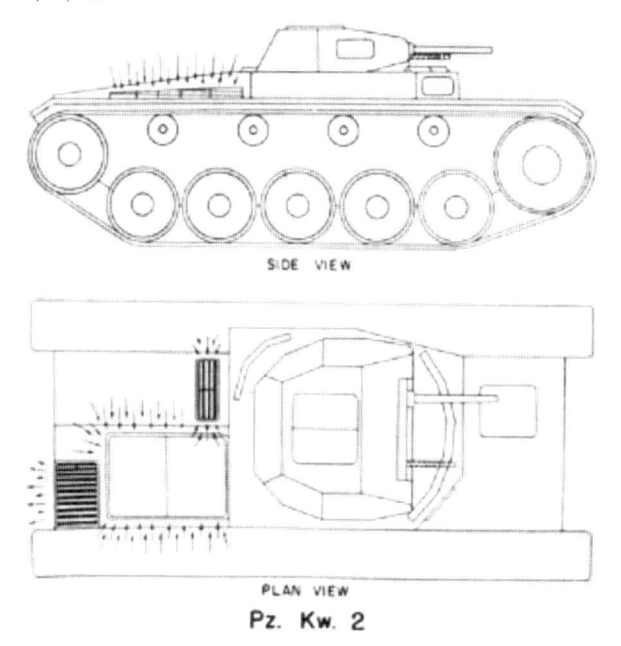

SIDE VIEW

PLAN VIEW
Pz. Kw. 2

SIDE VIEW

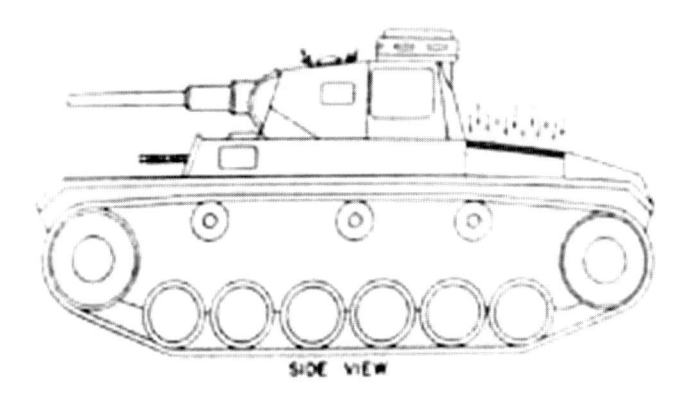

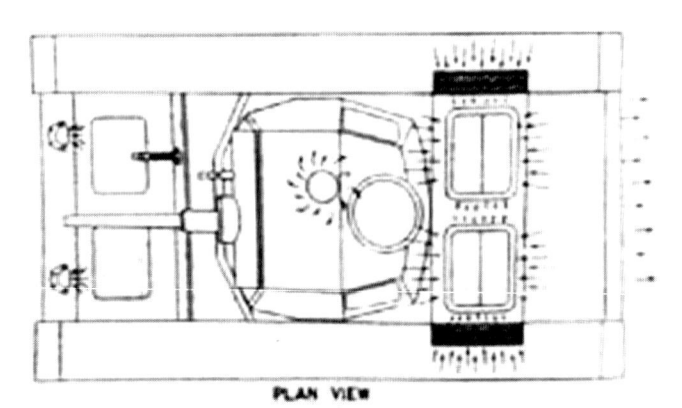

FRONT VIEW

PLAN VIEW

Pz. Kw. 3

SIDE VIEW

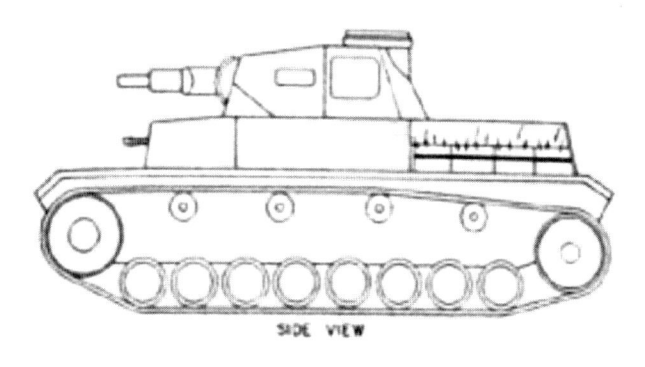

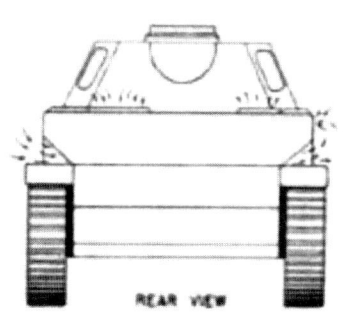

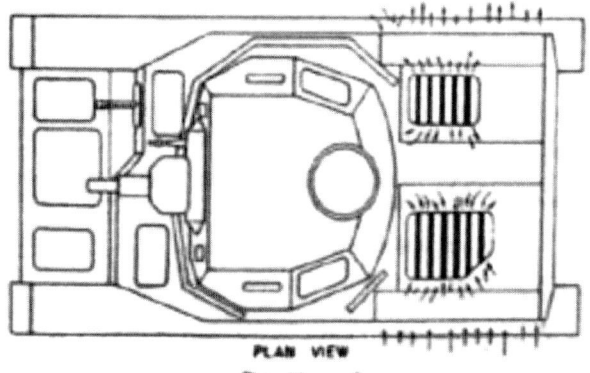

REAR VIEW

PLAN VIEW

Pz. Kw. 4

12. NIGHT COMBAT BY RUSSIAN CAVALRY

Intelligence Bulletin, October 1942

1. GENERAL

The Russians have proved that there is a definite place for horse cavalry in battle, despite the wide use of mechanized forces and airplanes in modern warfare. By operating at night, cavalry avoids attack by aircraft, and moves, dismounts, and strikes with much more surprise than during daylight hours.

2. METHODS OF ATTACK

The success of a night attack depends largely upon careful reconnaissance of the enemy positions. A commander's reconnaissance includes the approaches to the enemy's positions and the location of his firing points and outposts. Before nightfall, all steps have been taken to provide absolute secrecy of movement. The plan of every assault group is worked out in detail. Units are designated to seize outposts and guards, and deal with the automatic riflemen, the machine-gun crews, and the tank crews when they come out of bivouac.

In moving to the point from which the attack is to be made, the Russians do not fire a shot, unless the Germans open fire. In this case all Russian fire power is put into action.

Experience has taught the Russians that it is difficult for cavalry to use artillery in night operations, except while on the defensive. Normally, the cavalry regiments and squadrons take along their heavy machine guns in carts. The machine guns are capable of accomplishing the mission usually assigned to artillery. Antitank units are equipped with antitank weapons, grenades, and bottles of gasoline ("Molotov cocktails").

All equipment is carefully inspected before the cavalry leaves for the attack. Stirrups are wrapped with felt or straw. At a point about 3 to 5 miles from the enemy positions, the machine-gun carts are left in he open and the guns and mortars are carried in pack. The troops dismount again in open areas near the enemy outposts, and the horse-holders hide the horses.

If the mission is to seize a particular point, machine guns and mortars support the action without a let-up until the point is taken. If the mission is to destroy an enemy unit, the troops return when the mission has been accomplished. In this case the machine guns and mortars are placed in positions where they can also provide fire for the withdrawal of the units, in addition to supporting the attack.

These night attacks are planned so as to be completed 2 or 3 hours before daybreak. The Russians need this time interval in order to return to their original positions without being exposed to air attacks.

3. EXAMPLE OF TYPICAL ATTACK

The following is quoted from a Russian report as an example of typical cavalry night operations against a village:

"Two days were required to prepare this attack. The village was 22 kilometers (about 14 miles) from our division position. A troop had been sent out on reconnaissance. It went out on the highway, concealed itself in the forest, and observed road movements; it determined the enemy strength, location of outposts, and location both of tank parks and night bivouacs, as well as the headquarters and rear elements.

"The approaches to the town were important. West and south were two ravines too rough for tanks. The decision was to attack from the north and east. These directions would permit cutting off any attempt of the Germans to withdraw along the highway which ran north of the city. They would catch the enemy under crossfires and at the same time avoid danger of firing on our own troops. Since one regiment attacked from north and the other from east to west, this danger was averted.

"The division moved out in two columns at 1900; at 2400 it assembled 3 kilometers (about 2 miles) from the town, dismounted at once; and went into action. To insure surprise, the attack was made without the use of signals. The outguards were jumped without noise, and the units advanced on the bridge in the town. Here three German guards opened fire, but it was too late. Our troops threw grenades into the houses used as quarters, the assault groups attacked the firing positions, and 15 tanks were put out of action. The remaining tanks moved to the highway, but our engineer units had blown up the bridge. The fight ended at 0500, and from then until daylight (in December, about 0800) the troops returned to their position unnoticed by enemy aircraft.

"Our missions are usually for the purpose of opening the way for the infantry.

"As a result of these attacks, the Germans are now posting strong outguards, and even more careful reconnaissance is required.

"During such night attacks the Germans try to capture our horse-holders."

13. TANKS IN NIGHT ACTION

Tactical and Technical Trends, No 15, December 31st 1943

The following report is from an article by two Russian officers in Red Star, an official Russian newspaper. It describes how a German regiment was dislodged from a strong position during night fighting.

Until very recently the extent of night tank action on the front has been limited to night marches, negotiation of water obstacles, and movement to jump-off positions for attack. On the field of battle, the tanks participated only from dawn to dusk. The opinion prevailed that at night the tanks were blind and would therefore lose direction, bog down in natural and artificial tank obstacles, and would not be able to conduct aimed fire. However, recent battles on one sector have shown that the effectiveness of night tank action is well worth the difficult preparations involved. The following is a report on one night action.

An enemy regiment had defended two important hills for some time. From these hills, he had good observation of our positions, which were on the far side of a river. Our positions were continually kept under effective fire. The attempts of the Soviet infantry to capture the hills were in vain.

The commander decided to attack at night. Under cover of darkness, a tank unit was ferried across the river, and concealed in a grove. The following day was spent in reconnaissance, and coordination and establishment of communications. The commander decided to send the tanks on a flanking movement from the south and the southwest, in order that the impression would be created in the enemy that they were surrounded by a large force.

The tanks were echeloned in depth. The heavy tanks were in

the first echelon, the light tanks with "desyanti" (infantry mounted on tanks — see this publication, No. 3, p. 44) were in the second echelon, and in the third echelon were tanks hauling guns. The shells for the gun were carried on the tanks.

Three minutes before the attack, the artillery fired an intensive preparation on the front lines of the enemy, and then shifted to the rear, concentrating on the possible avenues of retreat. Zero hour was 30 minutes before dark. In these 30 minutes the tanks moved from the jump-off positions, reached the Soviet infantry positions, and moved out.

A full moon aided observation. After crossing the line of their own infantry, our tanks opened fire. The flashes of the enemy guns, and flares discharged by Soviet infantry aided fire direction.

The enemy artillery conducted unaimed, disorderly fire, and often shelled their own infantry. Pressed from both the flanks and the front, the enemy started a disorderly retreat. In 4 hours of battle, our tanks and infantry took full possession of the enemy strongpoint. After that the tanks maneuvered along the south and southwestern slopes of the hills, enabling our infantry to consolidate their positions. When it became evident that the hills were securely occupied by our infantry, the tanks returned to a grove to refuel, take on more ammunition and be inspected.

The German dead, the equipment left on the field of battle, and the prisoners captured that night gave proof that the night attack was a complete surprise to the Germans. The impression of complete encirclement was created, and enemy officers and men scattered in all directions. The enemy attempted a few counterattacks, but they were all beaten back.

In the following days, a few more night attacks were made on this and other sectors of the front. They were all successful and resulted in very few losses in Soviet tanks.

From the experience of these battles, the following conclusions can be drawn.

(a) The attacks must be made on moonlit nights, when the infantry can orient itself and give the tanks the signals necessary for them to maintain direction.

(b) The tanks must be used in echelons. This allows movement on a comparatively narrow front, and creates an exaggerated idea as to the number of tanks in battle.

(c) Having occupied a certain line, the tanks must continue their maneuver so as to enable the infantry to consolidate its positions.

During the attack, the tanks must under no circumstances be separated from the infantry. The tanks need the help of the infantry at night more than in the daytime.

14. TRAINING OF RUSSIAN AUTOMATIC RIFLEMEN

Tactical and Technical Trends, No 15, December 31st 1943

The following report, a translation of an article by a Colonel in the Russian Army, is believed to give the latest Russian thought on the training of the automatic rifleman. The Russian automatic rifleman here referred to is equipped with a weapon comparable to the Thompson submachine-gun. According to a Russian instructional poster, best results are obtained with this weapon as follows: single shot, up to about 300 yards; short bursts, about 200 yards; long bursts, about 100 yards.

The fundamental assignments of the automatic riflemen are:

(a) To break up, or throw into confusion, enemy battle formations by sudden assault fire, creating the semblance of encirclement where possible;

(b) To filter through the gaps between the enemy units, and cause heavy losses by striking at his flanks and rear;

(c) To disorganize enemy control by sudden assaults on his staffs and command posts;

(d) To capture and hold important strategic points (crossroads, railheads, bridges, etc.).

It may readily be seen that men required for such tasks must be trained primarily as attackers. They must be excellent athletes and bold fighters. Furthermore, they must be capable of self-sacrifice, and have the ability to operate under any weather conditions, in the daytime or at night. It is of prime importance that they remain cool under any battle conditions. Surprise is always the basis of their action. In many cases it is necessary to creep up to within 150 to 250 yards of the enemy without being detected, and open fire so as to throw the enemy ranks into confusion if not to wipe them out.

It is necessary to select candidates carefully for this specialty in the Red Army. The men must be physically well developed, as well as in perfect health, particularly as regards eyesight and hearing. Their will-power and determination must be of the highest caliber.

The program of training for automatic riflemen is drawn up with special consideration as to their battle functions. The individual training of the automatic riflemen approximates that of the infantry riflemen in the elementary stages. Emphasis is placed on the following:

(a) Thorough familiarity with the automatic rifle, to include reduction of stoppages and care in the field;

(b) Marksmanship, to include firing from all positions at stationary, moving, and surprise targets;

(c) Throwing of grenades and gasoline bottles, especially against tanks, embrasures, and trenches;

(d) Ability to ski;

(e) Self-orientation by azimuth, compass, or map at any time.

In the individual tactical training of automatic riflemen, 8 to 10 hours are devoted to courses in: "The Automatic Rifleman in Offense," "Actions of Automatic Riflemen in Attack and Inside the Enemy Defenses" and "The Automatic Rifleman in Defense." Stress is laid upon movement by rushes and crawling noiseless approach to enemy positions, use of camouflage, and utilization of cover. Each trainee must learn the various means of preparing satisfactory fire positions for prone, kneeling, sitting, and standing fox holes. He must also know how to fire from skis and tanks.

The unit tactical training includes courses in: "Action of Automatic Rifle Units in Attack and Inside the Enemy Defenses," "Action of Automatic Riflemen Accompanied by Tank Destroyers in Offense," "Night Attacks by Automatic Rifle Units," "Automatic Rifle Units in Defense," "Automatic Rifle

Units in Encircling Movements" and "Action of Automatic Rifle Units in Rear of the Enemy."

All studies should be conducted under practical conditions which approximate battle conditions as closely as possible, i.e., in snowfall, fog, poor visibility, etc. These studies should be filled with adverse situations to complicate operations, such as sudden assault from ambush, outflanking, appearance of enemy on the flanks or in rear, and encirclement.

Such practice develops initiative, cunning, "fight," and ability to think calmly under battle conditions. An automatic rifleman must never be allowed to forget that he may have to fight as an individual, separated from his unit, at any time and under any conditions. On the way to and from exercises, such factors as defense against aircraft, antitank defense, defense against motorized units, etc., are introduced and absorbed. Ability to dig in quickly, to pass through barbed-wire entanglements and other obstructions, and to work while wearing the gas mask, is emphasized.

In order to relieve monotony and to keep interest of the trainees alive, it is suggested that the different subjects be taught in varied, short lessons to achieve desired standards. A model daily lesson outlined early in the course consists of: complete assembly and disassembly of the automatic rifle; fire from cover; observation on the battlefield; discovery and choice of targets; study of grenades; and use of hand grenades.

Comment:

Although the actual number of automatic rifles in Red Army infantry units is not known, it is believed to be comparatively high. Before the war with Germany, there were at least two per rifle squad, and it is believed the number per large infantry unit has been increased.

The Soviet press has repeatedly emphasized the importance of automatic rifles. Many photographs taken at the front show whole units of automatic riflemen. The Red Army "desyanti" troops who ride the tanks are always pictured armed with this weapon. Pictures of junior officers with this weapon have been noted.

As the Red Army teaches "close-in" fighting, using short ranges, it is readily understandable why so much emphasis is placed on this weapon and on the training of men to use it in the proper manner. The above article deals with the ideal training which is striven for but not believed to be achieved. The average automatic rifleman is, of course, more highly trained than an infantry rifleman.

15. CAVALRY IN MASS

Intelligence Bulletin, May 1946

Soviet Doctrine for Employing Horse-Mounted Troops

Horse cavalry, like an insurance policy, is expensive but nice to have around when you really need it. In Russia, where horsemanship is part of the every-day life of many thousands of people, the Red Army is able to maintain one of the finest horse-mounted components in the world. Here is the doctrine with which Soviet cavalrymen rode to victory in World War II.

The Red Army, unlike the rest of the Allied powers, did not relegate the horse cavalry into the discard during World War II. Instead, Soviet Russia made effective use of its cavalry components, and even increased the number of horse cavalry units. The U.S.S.R. proved that the employment of horse cavalry as an independent striking force, and as a component of a cavalry-tank team, is clearly justified. The results obtained by Red Army cavalry units have proven the right of the almost legendary Cossack to remain part of the armed forces of the U.S.S.R. The lessons learned may well be studied by other countries.

Horse cavalry has always played a large part in Russian military campaigns. Russian cavalry forces have been known in every war in which Russia's troops have fought. During the reign of Czar Ivan the Terrible, a relatively small Cossack force under Ermak achieved the conquest and annexation of Siberia. The great distances, unmarked by roads, and the difficult terrain of that area were tailor-made for a cavalry operation.

Even to this day there large areas of flat plains and steppes in the U.S.S.R. that have only a limited network of roads. Easy traverse of these areas is feasible only to horses. Climatic conditions in Eastern Europe, especially during the spring thaws, place a very stringent limitation on all movement, except over first-class highways. Each spring the Ukraine, White Russia, and Eastern Poland become veritable seas of almost unbelievably deep mud. In consequence, cavalry has been an indispensable arm of the Red Army, even in this war of mechanized and motorized forces.

Since 1917, when the Red Army took over the forces of the Czar, the cavalry units of the Red Army have undergone many changes. Among other things, the over-all strength of the cavalry arm has been increased. During World War II, the Red Army had approximately 10 cavalry corps. Other changes have increased the fire power of cavalry units by adding mortars; more and heavier artillery, including self-propelled; more automatic weapons including submachine guns; and by making tank regiments an integral part of cavalry corps.

To be a cavalryman in the Red Army, a Soviet soldier does not have to be a Cossack. And, contrary to popular belief, the Cossacks have no monopoly over the cavalry arm. Cossack units, like the Kuban Cossacks (above), are recruited among the life-long horsemen of Kuban area of the U.S.S.R. But cavalrymen are also recruited from other areas, and although they may lack the glamour of the Cossack, they are none-the-less efficient soldiers. Such a non-Cossack cavalry unit is pictured below.

Further emphasis is placed on the Red Army evaluation of horse cavalry as a fighting arm by the establishment, since 1934, of 74 stud farms, geographically located to breed horses best suited to the locality. The farms are operated by the Red Army Remount Service.

Red Army cavalry organization differs considerably from the organization of U.S. cavalry units. Numerically, Red Army units are the smaller. A Soviet cavalry corps is roughly equal numerically to a reinforced U.S. horse cavalry division. Within the Red Army cavalry corps, also, are from two to four tank regiments as organic elements of the corps. The U.S.S.R. cavalry regiment is so designed as to provide a small and mobile striking force, heavily reinforced by supporting weapons. Numerically equal to less than half a Red Army infantry regiment, the U.S.S.R. cavalry regiment has almost as much fire power in supporting weapons.

In the cavalry corps, the artillery elements play no small part. The corps artillery commander has at his disposal five artillery regiments, armed with a variety of weapons. The type and relative numbers of artillery weapons are selected to achieve maximum flexibility and shock power without impairing the mobility of the corps. Including mortars and artillery of the cavalry divisions, the cavalry corps has nearly 350 pieces of artillery, plus several multiple rocket launchers. This is sufficient to throw, in a single salvo, a metal weight of more than 6 tons.

CAVALRY IN THE OFFENSE

Red Army doctrine stresses that cavalry should be used as an independent striking force; that cavalry is not a substitute for mechanized forces, but is a powerful force for operations where motorized units are handicapped by impassable terrain. By Red Army definition, cavalry is capable of taking part in every kind of engagement, and of carrying out actions of every type in cooperation with other arms; in addition to being able to operate independently.

Operating apart from other troops, horse cavalry attempts to strike the enemy flank or rear, to encircle and destroy the main body, and to cooperate generally with air forces, armored units,

The crew of an 85-mm SP gun and tank destroyer, on a T34 tank chassis, ride their weapon through a town in Rumania. These weapons are organic equipment of the two tank regiments within the Soviet cavalry corps.

T34 medium tanks on the road in Manchuria. Like the tank destroyers, they are the organic armored strength within the two tank regiments of the cavalry corps.

airborne units, and frontal assault groups. Other cavalry missions are large-scale raids, screening of troop movements of other arms, and counterattacks against the enemy flanks and far from concealed areas in the rear of a defensive position.

Cavalry can operate in very severe climatic conditions and over severely cut-up terrain. Over extremely difficult terrain, Red Army cavalry can average 5 miles per hour. Small units are unable to maintain continuous movement for long periods under combat conditions due to lack of organic transport and difficulty of resupply. Large units, however, with a sizeable supply train and an established resupply system, can operate for much longer periods and over long distances. One reinforced cavalry corps was given the mission of penetrating behind German lines and advancing for 60 miles parallel to the front and across the enemy lines of communication, thus effecting a junction with another cavalry corps in the area. The movement was entirely through forests and crosscountry in 2 feet of snow, with temperatures as low as 30 degrees below zero. In 6 days, the corps traveled 55 miles and captured large supplies of enemy matériel.

Red Army conception of cavalry raids extends to larger operations, over a longer period of time, and with a larger body of troops than is normally considered as a raid by U.S. doctrine. One raid made during World War II included a whole corps and lasted for 135 days, much of the fighting being behind the enemy lines.

In the breakthrough, Red Army cavalry was a valuable asset to the pursuit. When an enemy rear guard attempted to hold up the pursuit, the cavalry was able to make wide flanking movements through swamps and other difficult terrain to strike the retreating enemy in the flanks and to set up road blocks. In addition, the Soviets believe cavalry is useful in attacking enemy artillery and salient terrain features to protect highways along which armor and self-propelled artillery can then advance more easily.

It is a Red Army practice to detach small cavalry units from the main body to reduce by-passed strongpoints. Here the

A Tchanka machine gun cart for Maxim M1910 7.62-mm machine gun rolls across the steppes of Russia. This is a weapon of the cavalry heavy machine gun squad.

Cossack artillerymen, men of the 76.2-mm howitzer battery of a cavalry regiment, go into action in the North Caucasus

cavalry attacks dismounted from all sides, supported by their mortars and machine guns. Generally these detached units are of sufficient strength to reduce the strongpoint quickly so that they can rejoin the main body of cavalry troops.

Cavalry is used by the U.S.S.R., in conjunction with other arms, in the same manner in which it is used by other armies. Cavalry is used for reconnaissance, counterreconnaissance, screening, and patrol missions. The Soviets make extensive use of night cavalry reconnaissance and raids, particularly during winter weather.

With infantry, Red Army cavalry is used to great advantage. While the infantry holds the enemy with a frontal attack, the entire mass of cavalry and tanks are thrown in on the enemy flank and rear.

The best time to commit a cavalry force, the Red Army believes, is when an initial penetration of enemy defenses has been made by a frontal or enveloping attack. At that time, when the enemy is bringing up his reserves and his defenses are in a fluid state, the enemy has not had time to consolidate and organize any strong defensive position, and cavalry will encounter conditions that are conducive to success.

CAVALRY IN DEFENSE

In defense, Red Army cavalry is used to cover the withdrawal and to protect the flanks and gaps between units. In extreme conditions, the cavalry troopers dismount and engage in defensive combat as infantry. Care is always taken to conceal horses in a defiladed area for safety and to facilitate withdrawal. In the defense of road blocks or tactically important terrain, the organic artillery and mortars are the basic defensive weapons upon which the Soviet cavalry relies.

TRAINING

Immediately after the Russian Civil War, the cavalry forces were led mostly by ex-Czarist officers who joined the Red Army. Then an officer cavalry school was established to develop cavalry officers of proletarian origin. This school later became the

A Cossack cavalry patrol receives orders and instructions before departing on a reconnaissance mission. Red Army cavalry, unlike our own, carry their weapons slung on their back or chest, instead of in a rifle boot snapped to the saddle.

Don Cossack guardsmen, members of an elite Red Army cavalry regiment, rest in the foothills of the Carpathian mountains after action on the Second Ukrainian front. The broad-bladed sabre is the traditional weapon of these horsemen.

Buddennyi Red Army Cavalry Academy of Moscow, and is now the highest cavalry institute in the U.S.S.R. During the war there were nine cavalry officer training schools in operation.

Enlisted men and NCO's were trained in replacement cavalry regiments. There were 34 of these regiments during the war.

The cavalry courses at officers schools have ranged from 3 years in peacetime, prior to 1937, to 12 months during the war. Enlisted men serve 2 years in the cavalry army in peacetime. During the war, basic training for enlisted personnel lasted 8 months. During this time the enlisted man was trained in field tactics, individual weapons, elementary topography, care of horses and equipment.

CONCLUSION

The U.S.S.R., with vast distances and few roads, and with severe climatic conditions during much of the year, has used horse cavalry to great advantage during World War II.

By the results achieved, the Soviets have justified the use of cavalry, not as a substitute for armor and mechanized forces, but as an independent arm and as a supplement to armor and mechanized might in operations over severe terrain.

Russian cavalry has great power in supporting weapons. The organization is so designed as to provide a small and mobile striking force with adequate support of artillery, mortars, and automatic weapons. Cavalry and tanks have been combined into a smooth working and effective organization.

In World War II, as in most all of their other wars, the Russians were able to use large masses of horse cavalry, since much of the fighting took place within the borders or countries adjacent to their homeland. But over long distances, cavalry is not as economical. Transport of horses and equipment, especially ocean transport such as would have been necessary for the United States in the Pacific War, requires a large allotment of transportation facilities. In fact, the U.S. did maintain one horse cavalry regiment briefly in New Caledonia early in the war, but this unit was mounted on horses shipped from Australia. The unit existed as a horse-mounted organization only briefly, for it was eventually dismounted and sent into infantry action elsewhere in the Southwest Pacific. The only U.S. horse-mounted cavalry regiment to see action in World War II was the 26th Cavalry, a regiment of Philippine Scouts who covered the withdrawal of U.S. and Philippine forces to Bataan peninsula. This unit fought a classic cavalry rear-guard action from Lingayan to Bataan. Its mission was accomplished, although the regiment was virtually annihilated.

16. RUSSIAN ARTILLERY SUPPORT IN TANK ATTACKS

Tactical and Technical Trends, No 34, September 23rd 1943

The following article on artillery and tank cooperation in the attack is reproduced from the Soviet newspaper "Red Star."

When the fringe of the enemy defense has been broken and the leading formations advance to exploit their success, forward artillery observation is essential. Without this observation, fire from batteries in concealed positions will not be sufficiently effective to give continuous support to the advancing troops. The correct position of the artillery observer has, therefore, for some time, been with the leading elements of the infantry.

The problem, however, is to ensure powerful artillery support to mobile forces effecting a deep penetration. Single guns and gun troops accompanying these forces cannot always succeed in neutralizing enemy strongpoints of resistance. Tanks are either forced to stop or detour, with the result that the tanks are subject to serious threats from their flanks. Artillery time-tables prepared in advance, based only on reconnaissance data, are not sufficiently reliable, in view of the impossibility of discounting all the eventualities in battle.

Practical combat experience has proved that forward artillery observation is possible also in the case of thrusts delivered by tanks. This means that an artillery officer must be with the tanks forming part of the first wave. From this position, he will be able to judge what is holding up the advance; to call for and correct fire, and thus, although expending less ammunition, but achieving greater effect, the problem of providing fire support for advancing tanks is solved. At the same time, the possibility of shelling empty ground or one's own tanks is greatly reduced.

The experience gained by formations recently employed in the offensive on the (Russian) southern front allows for deductions of practical value.

In one case, an artillery regiment was allotted the task of supporting a tank formation which was to effect a deep breakthrough. The commander of the artillery regiment appointed one of his best officers, for liaison duty with the tank formation during the advance. Two days prior to the attack, this Russian officer became friendly with the tank crew allotted to him, learned how to fire the tank gun and machine gun, studied the probable course of the battle, arranged with his regiment the radio code procedure to be adopted for correction and control of fire, and checked the long and short wave lengths. From the beginning of the operation, he assumed command of the tank assigned to him.

As long as the tanks successfully dealt with targets with their own weapons the officer continued in his role of tank commander, and succeeded in destroying an enemy tank gun. Suddenly, however, the tanks came up against heavy opposition. The commander of the tank formation gave the order to move to a ravine for cover and allow time for straggling tanks to come up. The moment for fire support to assist the tanks had arrived. The artillery observation officer then transmitted his orders by radio. He directed and corrected the fire, as a result of which a concentration of two batteries succeeded in destroying the enemy points of resistance and permitted the tanks to continue their advance. Supporting fire was not restricted to opposition which was obstructing the advance of the formation to which the officer was assigned, but succeeded in providing assistance to formations advancing on his left flank which permitted the latter to fulfill their task.

A number of valuable lessons can be learned from this experience; first, the fact that forward artillery observation in mobile formations is effective is confirmed. As a result of the radio link the commander of the artillery is at all times aware of the position of the tanks and can provide coordinated and directed fire, taking fullest advantage of the range and trajectory.

This link is especially important when, due to weather, or other conditions, aircraft is unable to cooperate with mobile groups. Nevertheless, the organization of this type of forward observation required certain specific preparation. It is essential to assign as observer an experienced officer who is capable of orienting himself in any type of country.

Second, it is necessary to assign two observers to avoid any interruption should the tank of one of the observers be knocked out in action; furthermore, two observers enjoy a better view of the entire field of battle.

The position of the observer in the tank is usually beside that of the tank commander. Through him the observer can decide on various independent tasks, supplement and check the results of his personal observation and can restore communication with his artillery in the event of a break-down of his own radio set. It is emphasized that an observer should not maintain a position too far forward, from where the movement of the main mass of tanks cannot be properly followed. Observation is, furthermore, restricted, owing to the necessity of keeping the tank tightly closed.

The artillery officer is to be warned not to take too active a part as tank commander, and thereby lose sight of his main task. In pursuing individual objectives he may easily reduce his artillery to inactivity and the tanks will fail to receive support when needed. The observer's movements should be based on a careful and skillful maneuver giving him the best possible view of the field of battle, and he must remember that several dozens of guns are more effective than any one tank.

The method for calling for fire and correction is normal; by using a map previously encoded, the observer constantly pinpoints his position. On discovering a definite target he transmits by radio the nearest reference point and the relation of the target to it, at the same time indicating the type of concentration required. In adjusting the fire the observer indicates the correction in meters. The time of opening fire must be so selected as not to interfere with the movement of one's own tanks, unless these are halted in front of the target. The same principle is applied to the observer when putting down a barrage in front of his tanks or in parrying an enemy counterattack.

17. SOVIET INFILTRATION UNITS IN MOUNTAIN WARFARE

Intelligence Bulletin, June 1945

For Soviet troops engaged in combat in mountainous and forested areas, the Red Army advocates the use of small units to infiltrate through mountain defenses and harass an enemy's lines of communication. Although this tactic is not new - the Japanese have used it extensively in jungle fighting - the Russians, unlike the Japs, employ infiltration units as carefully coordinated parts of a general offensive operation designed to encircle and destroy mountain strongpoints and their defending troops.

These infiltration units may vary in size, a typical unit being composed of an infantry section or an infantry platoon. Such a unit is heavily armed with submachine guns or automatic rifles, a mortar, and possibly a machine gun or more. It is not unusual for engineers to be attached to a unit, their function being the

A typical infiltration unit is heavily armed with submachine guns or automatic rifles, a mortar, and possibly a machine gun or more.

No type of terrain is considered an obstacle, and full advantage is taken of routes over cliffs and other terrain features normally impassable.

reduction of obstacles which might impede the advance of the unit.

The Red Army conception of mountain warfare envisages the employment of large masses of troops, despite terrain. An enemy line of mountain strongpoints is softened by powerful artillery and air bombardment. Then, under cover of its own mortars and direct fire weapons, an infantry assault is launched in an endeavor to pin down the enemy defenses and perhaps secure a breakthrough.

It is during this assault, when the enemy troops are fully occupied defending their positions, that the infiltration units take advantage of unguarded terrain, or move through the breakthrough to establish themselves deep in the enemy rear area. No type of terrain is considered an obstacle, and full advantage is taken of routes over cliffs and other terrain features normally considered by the enemy to be impassable. Several infiltration units may move independently through the same general area.

The mission of these small groups is to emerge eventually in

Small patrols roam over a wide area, harassing indiscriminate targets in an effort to create the impression that a much larger force has penetrated the enemy rear.

Infiltration units occupy dominating terrain, and main roads are interdicted with small-arms fire until the enemy is forced to use secondary roads or to cease all movement temporarily.

a predesignated sector on the main supply and evacuation route in the enemy rear area. Here they occupy dominating terrain and endeavor to block all movement of supply and evacuation to and from the enemy mountain strongpoints. Small patrols roam over a wide area harassing indiscriminate targets in an effort to create the impression that a much larger force had penetrated to the enemy rear. Vehicles are wrecked and used as road blocks, and main roads are interdicted with small-arms fire until the enemy is forced to use secondary roads for communication, or to cease temporarily all movement to and from his front.

However, the Red Army realizes that small units cannot count on remaining unmolested once their harassing tactics become a serious threat. Consequently every effort is made to reinforce the groups with the continual infiltration of other such units until the strength of the Soviet troops behind the enemy lines grows progressively to a company. then a battalion, and finally a regiment.

The Red Army has discovered that by the time the infiltration has reached this stage, enemy supply operations have been seriously hindered, and resistance to assault upon his strongpoints has declined. It is then that an all-out Soviet assault must be launched, not only from the front and flanks of the positions, but from the rear by the now greatly reinforced infiltrated troops. Often, in such a situation, the enemy abandons his positions under the threat of encirclement. In such a case it is the mission of the infiltrated Soviet troops to attack and destroy retreating enemy groups. If the enemy stays to be encircled, the strongpoints are bypassed by the main strength of the assault, and are left to be liquidated by the encircling troops.

18. RUSSIAN TANK TACTICS AGAINST GERMAN TANKS

*Tactical and Technical Trends,
No 16, January 14th 1943*

The following report is a literal translation of a portion of a Russian publication concerning the most effective methods of fire against German tanks.

For the successful conduct of fire against enemy tanks, we should proceed as follows:

a. Manner of Conducting Fire for the Destruction of Enemy Tanks

(1) While conducting fire against enemy tanks, and while maneuvering on the battlefield, our tanks should seek cover in partially defiladed positions.

(2) In order to decrease the angle of impact of enemy shells, thereby decreasing their power of penetration, we should try to place our tanks at an angle to the enemy.

(3) In conducting fire against German tanks, we should carefully observe the results of hits, and continue to fire until we see definite signs of a hit (burning tanks, crew leaving the tank, shattering of the tank or the turret). Watch constantly enemy tanks which do not show these signs, even though they show no signs of life. While firing at the active tanks of the enemy, one should be in full readiness to renew the battle against those apparently knocked out.

b. Basic Types of German Tanks and their Most Vulnerable Parts

The types of tanks most extensively used in the German Army are the following: the 11-ton Czech tank, the Mark III, and the Mark IV. The German self-propelled assault gun

(Sturmgeschütz) has also been extensively used.

In addition to the above-mentioned types of tanks, the German Army uses tanks of all the occupied countries; in their general tactical and technical characteristics, their armament and armor, these tanks are inferior.

(1) Against the 11-ton Czech tank, fire as follows:
(a) From the front—against the turret and gun-shield, and below the turret gear case;
(b) From the side—at the third and fourth bogies, against the driving sprocket, and at the gear case under the turret;
(c) From behind—against the circular opening and against the exhaust vent.

Remarks: In frontal fire, with armor-piercing shells, the armor of the turret may be destroyed more quickly than the front part of the hull. In firing at the side and rear, the plates of the hull are penetrated more readily than the plates of the turret.

(2) Against Mark III tanks, fire as follows:
(a) From the front—at the gun mantlet and at the driver's port, and the machine-gun mounting;
(b) From the side—against the armor protecting the engine, and against the turret ports;
(c) From behind—directly beneath the turret, and at the exhaust vent.

Remark: In firing from the front against the Mark III tank, the turret is more vulnerable than the front of the hull and the turret gear box. In firing from behind, the turret is also more vulnerable than the rear of the hull.

(3) Against the self-propelled assault gun, fire as follows:
(a) From the front—against the front of the hull, the drivers port, and below the tube of the gun;
(b) From the side—against the armor protecting the engine, and the turret.
(c) From behind—against the exhaust vent and directly beneath the turret.

(4) Against the Mark IV, fire as follows:
(a) From the front—against the turret, under the tube of the gun, against the driver's port, and the machine-gun mounting;
(b) From the side—at the center of the hull at the engine compartment, and against the turret port.
(c) From behind—against the turret, and against the exhaust vent.

Remarks: It should be noted that in firing against the front of this tank, the armor of the turret is more vulnerable than the front plate of the turret gear box, and of the hull. In firing at the sides of the tank, the armor plate of the engine compartment and of the turret, is more vulnerable than the armor of the turret gear box.

19. "GERONIMO!" AND THE RED ARMY
Intelligence Bulletin, May 1946

"The use of paratroopers is a fine and intricate art, which is being developed by the Red Army not as a sport, but as a means of steeling personal courage, and as an important basis of our military power." Marshal Voroshilov, 1935.

Long before U.S. soldiers began stepping from aircraft in flight to cry "Geronimo!" as they floated earthward, the U.S.S.R. had a large body of trained paratroopers. In 1930, the Soviets began to experiment with sky soldiers, and in 1935 unveiled their troopers to the world in a mass jump of 1,200 men at Kiev.

In view of the fact that the Soviet Union was first in development of airborne troopers as a distinct striking arm, failure of the Russians to make adequate use of airborne forces in World War II is somewhat surprising. Paratroopers were used little, and Russian drops seem to have resulted in resounding failure.

No large-scale use of paratroopers, other than as elite infantry shock units in standard ground missions, was made by the Red Army with the exception of the drop of two brigades in 1943. Both brigades were almost entirely wiped out in this mission. Failure in this case was ascribed to the fact that the troopers were inadequately armed, and to insufficient training of the pilots making the lift. The troopers were dropped from too great an altitude, and were widely scattered. The equipment drops also failed.

The fact that the Russians made little use of airborne forces may be ascribed to several factors. For one thing, there was a critical shortage of aircraft, which were needed for other purposes, and there was a shortage of air crews trained in para drops. There was also a need to use the troopers as elite infantry in a purely ground role during the critical periods prior to 1944, and the airborne soldiers suffered very high losses in bitter combat, thus shortening the supply of experienced jumping personnel. Still another reason was the faulty registration of troopers trained prior to mobilization, with the result that many troopers were shunted into other type units when mobilization occurred.

Other missions carried out by Red Army paratroopers were generally on a small scale. Small parachute sections are believed to be attached to armies for espionage and sabotage purposes. Small groups of troopers have been used in cooperative roles with partisan groups behind enemy lines, and one entire brigade was dropped near Smolensk, in 1941, behind German lines. Many of the personnel in this drop were dressed in civilian clothing, and were expected to operate as Partisans.

Prior to World War II, the Soviet attempted, with very poor results, to use troopers in the Finnish war. In the occupation of Bessarabia, in 1939, paratroopers in the strength of a regiment of two battalions, totaling 2,000 men, were dropped ahead of the main forces to secure key points.

Beyond these small efforts the Russians did not go. It must not he inferred from their little active use of paratroopers in an airborne role that the Soviets do not consider them to he of distinct military value. On the contrary, there is much from which to infer the opposite. Experimentation is still going on, and troopers are considered as an elite body of troops. In 1945, Izvestia, a Soviet newspaper, carried a long story telling of the jump of a Lieutenant Colonel Amintaev from an altitude of over 34,000 feet. This same officer was credited, in the same article, with a total of 1,643 previous jumps. The article stated that Lieutenant Colonel Amintaev had made what appears to he the astounding total of 53 jumps in one day, in order to test the resistance of the human organism.

SPECIAL PRIVILEGES FOR JUMPERS

As in our own army, paratroopers in the Red Army enjoy the status of elite organizations, special privileges, and extra pay. The later-formed airborne organizations have been designated as "Guards" units. The "Guards" designation is normally given only to units after the unit has especially distinguished itself in combat. In the case of the airborne brigades formed later, however, the title of "Guards" has been given to the unit when it was organized.

In addition to physical ability, Russian paratroopers must come from parentage that is irreproachable in the communistic sense, and a large percentage are members of the Communist Party or of the Komsomol (Communist Youth Association). All those who, in the course of training, show a lack of will power are immediately transferred to infantry units.

For the most part, troopers are young. Officers are older than the troops, but are still the younger officers of the Red Army. The educational level of the members of the airborne brigades is higher than that of the infantry. According to regulations, enlisted men must have completed the 5th grade, and officers must have completed the 7th to 10th grade. By U.S. standard this may seem to be low, but by the standard of the average of the Red Army, it is quite high.

Extra pay, as received by the Red Army trooper, is based on the jump and the number of previous jumps completed. For the first jump, 25 rubles is paid in extra remuneration. For jumps 2 through 10, the sum of 10 rubles is paid for each jump. Jumps 11 through 25 are paid for at the rate of 25 rubles per jump.

Combat jumps are compensated for at a higher scale. Officers receive a whole month's pay for each combat jump, while noncommissioned officers receive 500 rubles and other enlisted men receive 300 rubles.

In order that bonus pay may be compared with regular rates of pay, the pay of a private of the Red Army may be considered to be 600 rubles per year, or approximately $120 per year. A rank similar to a private first class gets 1,000 rubles per year, or approximately S200. A sergeant receives 3,000 rubles per year, or approximately $600. Thus, for a combat jump, a sergeant would be paid the equivalent of a $100, a private would receive $60, or half a year's pay. A first lieutenant, who receives 7,700 rubles per year, or approximately $1,500, would receive for a combat jump a month's pay, or about the same amount that the private would receive as a normal year's pay.

Paratroopers enjoy privileges in the matter of food, also. A better ration is furnished the members of the airborne brigades than is general throughout the Red Army.

TRAINING PROGRAM

The course of training for the Red Army sky soldiers lasts approximately 4 months. During this period, the soldier receives a great deal of regular infantry training in weapons, tactics, signal communications, map reading, engineer training, artillery training, gas training, and maneuver. The parachute training comes in the second, third, and fourth months of the course. Each man makes five or six jumps before he is considered a trained parachutist, although he is awarded his parachutist emblem after his first jump. The first three jumps may be made from a captive balloon and the remainder from airplanes.

There is no special training school such as our own at Fort Benning, and training is given within the unit. There is, however, a special training center for officers, where the course lasts from 5 to 6 months. There, courses are graded according to rank and duties. It is interesting to note that some regular ground officers are detailed to these schools, and, in the course for platoon commanders, officers of the ground troops are trained on the same level as noncommissioned officers of the airborne brigades. This fact again speaks for the higher level of the airborne troops.

Many more officers are trained than are needed so that a definite selection of the better officers can be made, and it is often found that officers who have commanded battalions of infantry are found as company commanders in the airborne forces.

The physical condition of the men is good. Almost without exception they can endure the required day's march of 50 miles. Discipline is strict.

At the termination of the training period, large-scale combat exercises are held, with several brigades taking part.

ORGANIZATION

Within the Guards Airborne Brigades (Red Army short designation—VDV") the battalion is the tactical unit. The battalion consists of three rifle companies of 115 men each, one machine gun company of 89 men, one trench mortar battery of 92 men, one antitank rifle company of 112 men, and one platoon each of engineers, signal communications, and reconnaissance troops. Total battalion strength is 699 men.

Each VDV rifle company has four platoons of three squads each. Three platoons are rifle platoons and the fourth is a machine gun or mortar platoon. The mortar company is equipped with six 82-millimeter mortars.

The VDV brigade consists of four battalions of the organization detailed above, with a headquarters containing a gas platoon, medical section, and band. VDV brigade strength is between 3,500 and 4,200 men.

Officers, noncommissioned officers, and certain designated men are armed with submachine guns. Officers also are equipped with a pistol. Other men, with the exception of special "sharpshooters who are armed with special sharpshooter rifles, are armed with rifles or carbines. Hand grenades are handed out in unlimited number.

Each rifle company is equipped with nine light machine guns and three 50-millimeter mortars.

"STAND IN THE DOOR!"

Operational jumps are done at night. In particularly urgent cases, day jumps may be made by small parties, but it is not done if it can be avoided. Jumping altitudes are from 500 to 1,000 feet for day jumps, and from 1,300 to 1,900 feet at night.

The time necessary to release a stick of jumpers varies with the type of plane used and the degree of training of the jumpers. With one type plane, 18 men may be dropped in 18 to 20 seconds, though the Russians emphasize that poorly trained men may require as much as 90 seconds to clear the plane. With another type plane, 15 well-trained men may be dropped in 5 to 7 seconds. Some Soviet planes used for airborne drops are equipped with double doors and jumpers leave the plane from both sides.

Parachutes used by enlisted men are generally square cotton chutes with an area of approximately 70 square yards. It is semiautomatic in operation, and is also equipped with a handle release for emergency use. Enlisted men do not use reserve chutes.

Lined up for pre-jump inspection, these Red Army troopers wear regular infantry dress. Several types of chutes may be seen. In general, enlisted men do not use reserve chutes except on qualifying jumps.

Officers use a round chute, also of cotton, with approximately the same area as that used by enlisted men. It also is equipped for both hand and semiautomatic operation. Officers, however, are equipped with a silk reserve chute.

In training, the "PD-6" chute is used. This is the same chute used by officers. For operational jumps, however, the square "PD-41" chute is used, since it can be jumped from much lower altitudes than can the PD-6 because of its faster opening action.

The square parachute of the Red Army is equipped with a "köli" (keel), which is arranged by the jumper to turn the chute into the wind, and which cuts down on oscillation or swinging, thus making a very stable chute.

A cotton chute with a load capacity of approximately 250 pounds is the standard equipment chute. Other types are used for special equipment.

The uniform of the VDV soldier is the same as that for regular Red Army infantry, though paratroopers are issued only new clothing. There is also a special parachute infantry coat which has a fur collar and which is covered with a waterproof fabric.

The mission of airborne troops is considered by the Soviets to include the following: supporting the advance of their own troops; cutting the enemy routes of retreat; blocking the enemy reserves; isolation or destruction of enemy headquarters and rear echelons; the capture of key points; the forming of bridgeheads; capture of staffs and the capture of airplanes; and the protection of sea landings by securing stretches of coast line.

For small groups, missions are considered to be the execution of reconnaissance, sabotage work, and the support of Partisan groups.

Great emphasis is placed on cooperation with Partisans by airborne groups. Paratroopers are expected and encouraged to operate as Partisans themselves when the primary mission is accomplished. Indeed, the primary mission may be that of reinforcing Partisan groups, or Partisan operations only.

These troopers, trained in winter warfare, reflect the hardy physical specimens selected for elite airborne units. All are armed with submachine guns, though such is not the normal distribution of weapons in the airborne brigades.

WINTER WARFARE

The Soviets note that the large-scale employment of paratroopers may especially be used to advantage in winter, particularly in forests and mountain terrain. To this end, many VDV units are trained and equipped with skis. These are dropped with the men, or later at the place of assembly.

The VDV troops are trained in taking advantage of snow cover and severe cold in executing their mission. Emphasis is placed on the fact that security troops are normally placed on the roads during winter, thus ski-equipped paratroopers may make quick, surprise assaults on the flanks of a main body.

Troops are warned about using the same trail twice. They are instructed in doubling back on their own trail to set an ambush, leaving false trails, and other means of hiding their true route and ultimate destination from discovery by observation of ski trails.

VDV troops are given training in living in severe cold, and in means of improvising shelter. They are also given training in first aid in severe cold.

ASSEMBLY PATTERN

That bug-a-hear of all parachute operations, quick assembly on the ground, is provided for in Russian training. In order to cut scattering to a minimum, extraordinary precautions are taken. Lighter men are dropped first in the stick, and heavier men last, in attempting to concentrate the landing area. The Soviets expect that an average plane load will be landed in an area approximately 200 yards by 100 yards under normal conditions.

The normal method of assembly is as follows: The first men to jump go 50 yards in the direction in which the plane was flying. The last men, upon landing, go 50 yards in the opposite direction. In between they would normally find the other jumpers. They assume that it will take about 20 minutes to assemble a plane load in this manner.

Platoons are normally jumped from two planes which fly closely together to minimize scattering and drift. Assembly of a platoon is assumed to take 50 minutes.

Assembly of a company is carried out with the accent on preventing the enemy from determining the place of assembly.

Paratroopers may be extremely effective in executing sabotage missions in the enemy rear. These troopers are preparing to blow rails on an enemy supply line after skiing from the drop zone. Soviet troopers are trained in winter warfare.

Prior to the jump, the company commander informs his company of the assembly area. Immediately after landing, the company commander proceeds to that area, where he leaves a man with instructions for the platoons. The instructions may be something on the order of "3 miles, azimuth of 90 degrees." At the second place, the company commander leaves guides.

As the platoons are assembled individually under the control of the platoon leader, the man stationed at the initial assembly area gives the platoon leader the instructions. The platoon then proceeds to the second area where the guide meets them and guides them to the third and final assembly area. In each of the first two assembly areas, the guides may use a weak flash to signal their position to the others, but at the third and final area no such signal is made. This procedure safeguards disclosure of the company assembly point if some of the men should fall prisoner.

The battalion normally does not assemble, but the company commander, or his representative, goes to a predesignated spot from which they are guided to the battalion staff. There they get their orders, while their companies wait in their individual assembly points, or move in the direction previously ordered by the battalion order. Under certain circumstances the company may receive its final operational order before the jump, but this is not the usual practice since the Soviets go to great lengths to keep the operation secret. In some cases, the men have not even been told they were on an operation, and have thought, until landing, that they were on practice missions.

The Russians assume that it will take 4 hours to assemble the entire battalion after landing.

Since, in combat operations, scattering is normally greater than in training maneuver, and the orderly assembly may be interfered with, the assembly may be done differently. Special signals may be devised for assembly. Voice signals, special light signals, and all kinds of other signals such as smoke, flares, etc., may be used.

Equipment bundles are dropped, whenever possible, in the center of a stick landing area. Baggage is often dropped before the men, some of it without chutes. If it is not within the landing area, the men are instructed to form into a chain with 5 yards between each man to sweep the area.

Once assembled, normal infantry tactics are used. The tactical unit is the battalion. The company seldom is used on independent missions.

NOT FORGOTTEN

At this time, there is little information available on airborne forces as distinguished from purely parachute organizations. What part the glider and air-landed troops play in the Russian organization is still largely a matter of conjecture. It is known that there are provisions for glider forces in the Red Army. In 1935, an entire division was transported by air from Moscow to Vladivostok. Included in this air movement were some light tanks. The Germans seemed to believe that the Soviets are

These members of a Red Army parachute organization are machine gunners and are equipped with Degtyarev light machine guns, Model 1928. Some of the weapons are equipped with flash hiders, while the gun at lower right is fitted with a muzzle-cap.

instituting a light tank battalion in the new VDV brigades.

The organization and role of Russian parachutists has continually changed since the first large mass public jump in 1935. In the late years of World War II, the new VDV brigades were organized with a cadre from a small group of higher ranking officers and a few previously trained paratroopers. Most of the latter were salvaged from hospitals where they had been sent as the result of wounds suffered in normal ground combat operations. Since that time, provision has been made to train new men and to retain control over them by the airborne forces.

Continuing interest has been shown since the organization of the VDV brigades. It is probable that more changes will take place in organization and tactics on the basis of the slight war experience of the Soviets, and on the basis of what information is available about U.S. and British airborne operations.

The Russians have long realized the potentialities of vertical envelopment—longer than have the other nations. It is not likely that they will neglect an arm which has shown itself to be of high value in certain situations, both defensive and particularly offensive. It is probable that airborne troops will remain an elite force within the Red Army, and a force which must be soberly considered in any estimate of the Soviet military potential.

20. RUSSIAN TANK CAMOUFLAGE IN WINTER

Tactical and Technical Trends, No 17, January 29th 1943

The following report is a translation of a Russian article on tank camouflage in winter. The original article was written by a colonel in the Russian Army.

a. General

Winter camouflage of tanks presents a problem with certain special features, created on the one hand by the general winter background, and on the other by weather conditions which greatly affect the tanks themselves and their employment under combat conditions. In winter the change in the operational characteristics of the tanks and in the conditions of employing them in combat will influence the work to be done toward camouflaging them.

Winter conditions (as has been shown by combat experience) create considerable difficulties for the camouflage of tank units. In winter the principal characteristics of a region are its uniform white background, a lack of outline, and an almost complete absence of color. The only exceptions are small settlements, woods, and thick underbrush. Forests whose dense foliage provides perfect concealment in the summertime lose their masking qualities completely in the winter. In winter, on an even, white blanket of snow, camouflage is very difficult. Almost all methods of camouflage employed in summer prove inapplicable. It is necessary to make wide use of special winter covering for the vehicles, and to paint them with winter paint: all one color (protective coat) or in large spots (disruptive).

In winter, tracks made by moving vehicles can be easily recognized, not only from the air but also from high ground observation posts. The removal of tracks left by tanks is the personal responsibility of the commander of the tank units and of the crews. The presence of a blanket of snow, which is often very thick, greatly reduces the mobility of tanks, and as a result reduces the possibility of tanks appearing quickly and suddenly from directions unexpected by the enemy. Tanks cannot go through more than 3 inches of snow without appreciable loss of speed. The deepest snow through which a tank can go is 3 feet; for practical purposes tanks can operate in 1 1/2 feet of snow. It is apparent that these conditions greatly reduce the possibility of using approach routes concealed from enemy observation. Snow makes it necessary for tanks to employ existing roads, which means that they must engage in all their combat operations in those parts of the terrain which are under the special observation of the enemy.

An important winter factor from the point of view of concealment is the longer period of darkness, which helps to conceal the movement and disposition of tanks, provided, of course, that all camouflage measures are carefully observed.

Another winter factor which may be considered important from the point of view of camouflage and concealment is the greater cloudiness of the sky, which hinders reconnaissance activity by enemy aviation and sometimes stops it completely. Then too, tanks may make use of snowstorms which produce conditions of bad visibility and audibility, and as a result tend to lessen vigilance on the part of enemy observation posts.

b. Tank Painting

In winter, tanks are painted all white when the aim is to avoid observation, and in two colors with large spots when the aim is to avoid identification. As a rule, all-white paint is employed in level, open country characterized by a lack of variegated color. Two-color disruptive winter paint is used where the ground presents a variety of color, where there are forests, underbrush, small settlements, thawed patches of earth, etc.

One-color camouflage paint is applied to all parts of the tank in one or two coats. For the paint, zinc white or tytanium white is used only with an oil base, and slight amounts of ultramarine coloring. For the lack of anything better, the tanks may be painted with chalk dissolved in water.

Painting in two colors with large spots can be undertaken in two ways: one is to paint only part of the tank surface, leaving about 1/4 or 1/3 of the tank's surface in the original green; another is to repaint the tank entirely in two colors, either white and dark gray, or white and gray-brown.

When the weather is cold, painting should take place in a warm place, since paint applied when the temperature is 10° below zero Fahrenheit is too hard to be applied.

In winter, as in summer, it is necessary to avoid mechanical repetition of patterns and colors. For example, in painting the tanks of a platoon, one or two tanks are painted white, a third in white irregular stripes leaving parts of the protective green paint as it is, the fourth with white and dark gray spots, and finally, the fifth with white and grayish-brown spots.

c. Covers and Ground Masks

For winter tank camouflage, one may use nets made of cord which have fastened to them irregular white patches of fabric, about 1 yard across. A large all-white cover also may be used.

When using white winter covers, it is necessary to pay attention to the degree of whiteness of the materials used, for even if a little yellow shows or if part of the material is soiled, it will sharply outline the cover and the tank against the background of pure white snow. A simple method to improve this camouflage is to place a thin layer of snow on the cover.

In winter, ground masks are also used. But the construction of these camouflage masks involves special considerations dependent on the character of the background. The principal camouflage materials employed are irregularly shaped pieces of white fabric or painted white matting. In addition to the white patches, dark patches should be fastened to the material to give the appearance of bushes, tree tops, or other natural ground features. For dark patches one may use tree branches and other similar materials. As with covers, the use of white patches alone, or of a combination of white and dark patches, will depend entirely on the terrain and the coloration of the surroundings.

To attach the patches to the mask, they are frozen on after wetting the material with water.

d. Dummy Tanks

Drawing the attention of the enemy to dummy tanks has the same aim in wintertime as in summer, namely, to deceive the enemy concerning the disposition, types, and character of tank activity. However, in winter the making of dummy tanks is subject to certain special conditions. Large dummy snow tanks may be made by packing snow into the form of a tank, showing the hull, the suspension system, and the turret, and then spraying with paint. Movable life-size models are constructed not on wheels but on skis. "Flat" models may be made simply by treading the snow into the contours of a tank. In all other respects the making and use of dummy tanks in winter is no different than in summer.

e. Camouflage while in Motion

Generally speaking, winter conditions make it necessary to move along existing roads. Since winter roads appear to the aerial observer as dark strips, tanks which have an all-white winter paint stand out fairly clearly. In view of the fact that vehicles can be spotted by the shadow they cast, they should move on the side of the road nearest to the sun so that their shadow falls on the road, which is darker than the snow next to the road. Movement along the roads, especially at great speeds and over fluffy dry snow, gives itself away by clouds of snow dust. For this reason, movement of vehicles in wintertime should be at low speeds, especially over new-fallen snow. The tracks left by the tank treads stand out clearly as two dark parallel strips with tread impressions. These can be obliterated by sweeping the road. When tracks are left on the hard crust of the existing road it is necessary, instead of sweeping, to remove them with the aid of graders.

When the tanks pass through places where turns are unavoidable, there appear everywhere little heaps of upturned snow; these are characteristic marks and betray the movement of tanks. To prevent this, turns must be made gradually in a wide arc whenever practicable, or else the heaps of snow which are formed must be cleared away.

The reflection from the lenses of the tank headlights will also give away their movement. In order to prevent this, it is necessary to cover the headlights with white fabric covers, or some other material.

Finally, among the most important factors betraying the movement of tanks to ground observers is the clank of the tracks. [Russian tanks tracks are of all-metal construction.] The noise of these can be heard better as the temperature falls. Naturally, when operations are in the immediate vicinity of the enemy, one makes use not only of all the ordinary precautions employed in summer for the prevention of noise, but takes into account the special characteristics of winter weather with its increased transmission of sound.

f. Camouflage of Stationary Tanks

In winter, tanks are, generally speaking, parked alongside buildings and in woods and shrubbery; in exceptional cases it may be necessary to station tanks in open flat country or in gullies.

The peculiar characteristic of inhabited areas in wintertime from the point of view of camouflage is the motley appearance of the landscape due to the presence of dwelling places, barns, gardens, roads, and paths. This wealth and variety of outline affords considerable opportunities for concealing the position of tanks from air and ground observation by the enemy.

As a rule, all vehicles in bivouac should be placed under the roofs of sheds and barns. Only where there is an insufficient number of such structures, or where the size of the vehicles makes it impossible to place the vehicles in the existing shelters, is it necessary to build shelters, resembling the existing structures in the given locality. The roofs of these shelters must be covered with a layer of snow so that they will not look any different from the roofs of the existing structures. Just as in summertime, these camouflage structures may be built either as additions to existing structures or as separate structures. The separate camouflage structures should be situated along laid-out paths, and the tracks of the caterpillars which lead to the place where the tanks are stationed should be swept or dragged so as to resemble an ordinary road.

When there is not enough time to construct shelters, it is sometimes possible (as on the outskirts of a village) to camouflage tanks by simulating haystacks, piles of brushwood, stacks of building materials, etc. This is done by strewing over the vehicle a certain quantity of material at hand and covering it with a thin layer of snow.

Woods, orchards, and brushwood can be used for camouflage purposes in the wintertime only if additional camouflage precautions are taken. Since leafy woods offer much less concealment in winter than in summer and do not hide the vehicles from air observation, they must be covered with white covers, and there should be strewn over them broken branches or some other camouflage material such as hay, straw, etc.

When there are no white covers, the vehicles may be covered with dark ones, but snow must be placed on top and scattered. Dark covers can be used only against a background which has natural black spots. Finally, if no covers of any kind are available, the vehicles should be covered with branches, straw, hay, and the like, and snow placed on top in irregular patches.

When the tanks are stationed in open flat country, then the camouflage of the tanks also involves the breaking up of the uniform aspect of the locality, which is done by treading around on the snow. Then these areas are given irregular form by scattering here and there patches of pine needles, straw, and rubbish. The ground should also be laid bare, as tanks which are painted a dark color will not be easily discovered against a dark background, either by visual air observation or by the study of aerial photographs.

In open country, thaws are particularly favorable to camouflage of tanks, for the disappearing snow exposes portions of the surface of the ground. The result is that the ground assumes a naturally mottled appearance, and the contours of vehicles stationed there are easily blended. When there is deep snow, tanks may be placed in snow niches built near snowdrifts along the road. The entrances to these should be directly off the road in order to avoid tell-tale tracks of the treads. On the top the niches are covered with white covers, or with some other available material over which snow is placed. In order to camouflage the entrance, it is necessary to use hangings of white cloth or painted mats which may be readily let down or pulled up.

When the tank is stationed in a gully, it is covered with solid white covers of any kind of fabric or matting painted white, or by the regulation net, with white and black patches attached to it.

21. ON THE WAY!
Intelligence Bulletin, May 1946

The Employment of Mortars in the Red Army

Mortars, the infantryman's artillery, played a far greater tactical role in the Red Army than they did the U.S. Army as a supplementary weapon, with fire control decentralized to a small infantry unit, mortars in the Red Army were fundamentally used for massed fire as an independent striking weapon. From 1942 onwards, the large-scale use of mortars was developed into a definite tactical doctrine among Soviet troops. The US intelligence Bulletin of May 1946 carried an excellent overview of the use of mortars.

"Although fire requirements were set by the Red Army infantry, technical control and coordination are the responsibility of an artillery commander. Field artillery methods are used by Soviet mortar troops, who conduct massed fire missions for antitank-antipersonnel barrages, countermortar fire, and interdiction. They also will fire smoke missions, or in support of automatic weapons.

In the Red Army, mortars are classed either as light, medium, or heavy. The light mortar, a 50-mm equivalent of our own 60-mm mortar, is the standard weapon of the rifle company, there being a two-mortar platoon to each company. These mortars may either support their own company in action, or all the mortar platoons in a battalion may be combined into a six-piece provisional mortar company which fires missions in support of the whole battalion. In such a case, a fire direction center will be established, and fire conducted through the use of messengers and visual signals. Where possible, 50-mm mortar fire is coordinated with that of the medium mortar units.

The Soviet medium mortar is an 82-mm piece, the equivalent

The crew of an M1941 50-mm mortar go into action during one of the Red Army's winter offensives. Although normally the weapon of a mortar platoon, the platoons within a battalion may be combined to form a provisional mortar company.

of our own 81-mm mortar. Each battalion 82-mm mortar company, with nine pieces, may fire in support of its own rifle battalion. It is normal practice, however, when on the defense or in a static situation, to combine the three medium mortar companies of a rifle regiment into a provisional battalion

The crew of an M1938 82-mm mortar displace forward to a new firing position. In a fast-moving situation, the aggressive displacement of guns is one of the characteristics of Red Army mortar tactics

commanded by the regimental heavy mortar battery commander, whose pieces operate jointly with those of the three mortar companies. This provisional mortar battalion establishes a fire direction center with wire communication to observation posts, and to platoons through their company command posts. Observation posts are numerous, there being platoon OP's and company OP's in addition to those maintained by the battalion. The provisional battalion commander is in turn under the command and coordination of the division artillery headquarters. Thus the provisional medium mortar battalion, unlike our own decentralized control of 81-mm mortar platoons, may fire massed concentrations in support of the entire regimental front, or may on occasion fire into the sectors of adjacent regiments, range permitting.

The Soviet standard heavy mortar is the 120-mm, there being seven of them in the regimental mortar battery. There is no equivalent organization or weapon in the U.S. Army infantry regiment. In 1942, the Red Army organized some GHQ mortar battalions and regiments that function much as do our own 4.2-inch chemical mortar battalions.

CONDUCT OF MORTAR FIRE

Mortar troops of the Red Army conduct their fire according to a thorough procedure. Artillery intelligence is acquired aggressively, with platoons, batteries, and battalions, working with infantry and artillery patrols to push their OP's as far forward as necessary. Enemy information is carefully and thoroughly evaluated, and intelligence is exchanged by all echelons from field armies to mortar companies. Artillery intelligence reports, as issued by the artillery headquarters, contain the operational recommendations and requirements of even the lower echelon mortar units.

Based upon this intelligence, and upon a thoroughly developed firing technique, a comprehensive fire plan is established. Once established, the plan is not static, but changes continuously as the operational requirements of the supported rifle troops vary. Once in action. mortar units will determine the requirements of fire against various targets, make fire reconnaissance against minefields, register specific concentrations, and establish check points. Such preliminaries having been established, mortar units then concentrate on secrecy, surprise, aggressive displacement of guns, maneuver of fire, and varying their mortar tactics.

Constant coordination and liaison between the mortar units,

the artillery command, and the rifle units is a strict rule. The result is a closely knit fire plan wherein a single system of terrain reference is maintained by all troops. This in turn facilitates the requests for fire by rifle units, and its delivery by any or all fire support units.

Officer supervision and centralized control of mortar batteries is stressed in the Red Army by assigning a larger number of officers to mortar units than will be found in the equivalent units of the U.S. Army. Also. the greater number of medium and heavy mortars found in the Soviet rifle division, give it a striking power, by weight of projectile, of two and a half that of an American infantry division.

THE MEDIUM MORTAR COMPANY

Although medium (82-mm) mortar platoons may be assigned to separate support missions, or medium mortar battalions may be formed for massed fire under certain operational circumstances, the medium mortar company is the standard operational unit among Red Army mortar troops.

When on the offense, the medium mortar company must supply supporting fire for the most forward rifle battalion troops. During the general artillery preparation that precedes a Red Army infantry attack, the mortars concentrate on neutralizing enemy infantry positions, and breaking gaps through minefields and wire entanglements. As the Soviet infantry deploys, the mortars join with the artillery in providing general covering fire, and during the attack the mortars fire concentrations against the foremost enemy positions, known weapons emplacements, and counterattacking infantry.

When on the defensive, Soviet mortar companies, besides providing the normal support fires, must be prepared to put concentrations on concealed approaches anywhere within a mile and a half range, fire barrages to separate counterattacking enemy infantry from their tanks, and neutralize enemy forward

When on the offense, the medium mortar company must supply supporting fire for the most forward rifle battalion troops. Here the crew of an M1941 82-mm mortar move to a new position during the battle for Stalingrad.

support weapons. If enemy troops break into the Soviet defenses, the Soviet mortars are expected to aid in the destruction of these enemy elements by cutting off their path of retreat, and supporting the Red Army counterattack.

The Red Army mortar company moving into action is preceded by a reconnaissance section from the company, which selects the firing positions and observation posts. Whenever possible, the company OP is established near or in the same locality as the rifle battalion OP, since the mortar captain and the battalion commander maintain the closest liaison. Meanwhile, each mortar platoon establishes its own OP in front of its position, but not too far to prohibit the passing of verbal orders or signals from the OP's to the platoons. Telephone communication is established from each of the platoon OP's to the rifle battalion OP, and from there to the mortar company headquarters hack at the firing position. There is also wire communication between the battalion OP and the battalion command post.

When the company moves into its firing position, the usual

Members of a battalion medium mortar company set up an M1941 82-mm mortar among the ruins of Kharkov. The distance—about 35 yards—between this crew and the one in the background is SOP in the Red Army for medium mortars going into battery.

procedure is to deploy the platoons in line with no more than about 35 yards between platoons, each platoon front also being approximately 35 yards. Thus the mortars would be roughly dispersed in battery along a front of between 150 to 200 yards. This procedure varies with the terrain, of course, and mortar platoons may often be arranged in echelon, rather than line, but along a general, common front.

As the pieces are moved into position, a company base piece is designated, it usually being the mortar farthest to one flank. In turn, base pieces are designated for each platoon, again usually a piece on the flank of the platoon. The mortars are then laid to fire a parallel sheaf; that is, each mortar is laid to fire on the same azimuth. This is done by setting the platoon base pieces in parallel with the company base piece, usually by using an artillery aiming circle. Then the mortars of each platoon are laid in parallel with their respective base pieces, usually by reciprocal laying.

When the company firing position has been established, the company commander, his second in command, a telephone operator, and an observer from each platoon make a reconnaissance for an alternate firing position and observation posts. However, if the company is continually displacing forward to accompany rifle troops on the offensive, each platoon may reconnoiter and advance independently with the infantry company it is supporting. But in the more stable situation, the company commander may select a reserve firing position not less than 200 yards from his mortars, have mortar positions prepared at this alternate location, and have camouflaged communications trenches dug between the two localities.

After the company's sector of fire has been designated, probably by the artillery staff, the company commander prepares the company firing data with the aid of his observer. From five to seven reference points are selected in the company's sector, one of these being designated as the base point. Among these reference points are those which have also been selected by the rifle battalion commander for his own purposes.

It is not unusual for the mortar company commander then to assign separate fire missions to his platoons, particularly if

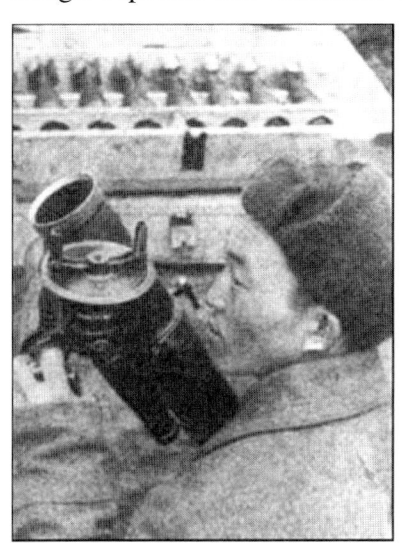

Red Army mortarmen lay their guns much the same way we do, however the sight they use may be either simpler or more complicated than our own. The sight on the 82-mm mortar (left) may be used for laying a parallel sheaf among mortars in battery.

Red Army mortarmen fall in for inspection at a Soviet training camp. The M1941 50-mm mortar, here shown in carrying position, is a weapon of the rifle company.

several targets have previously been marked for destruction. In such cases, platoon commanders prepare additional firing data of their own, including such things as range determination, charge selection, and the determination of angle of fire and deflection shifts. But when the whole company fires a concentration on one target, the preparation of firing data again becomes the responsibility of the company commander.

Registration on base points, reference (check) points, planned concentrations, etc., is by observed fire using the bracket method. This is done by the company commander using his base piece, firing first on the base point. Successive corrections are made during registration until the ratio of overs to shorts in a narrow fork does not exceed two to one in successive bursts. Then the sheaf is adjusted by firing all pieces at the determined range. On occasion, the ladder method is also used. During fire for effect, transfers of fire are computed from base points or from previous targets. Smaller sectors, or individual targets, may be designated to platoons, which then will register independently.

When in action, the company commander generally conducts the fire when his whole company is engaged on a single fire mission. However, if several targets are engaged at the same time, targets and fire missions may be allotted to the different platoons, in which case the platoon leaders will conduct the fire for their own pieces.

The Red Army medium mortar company is capable of laying a fixed barrage across a front of about 275 yards. It is the usual Soviet practice to allot 14 rounds per piece when conducting such a fire mission. Action is begun by firing two company concentrations of three rounds each, followed by four platoon salvos at 5-second intervals.

Defensive barrages against tank-borne infantry attacks are fired according to a prearranged plan. A series of phase lines between 300 and 400 yards apart are selected along the expected route of approach, the closest phase line being about 300 yards from the forward friendly positions. The ranges of each of these phase lines are determined in advance, and fire begins at the furthest phase line at the moment the lead tanks cross it. Fire is then shifted to each succeeding phase line until the attack is either repulsed, or has penetrated the last line.

Zone fire is conducted against enemy assembly areas and troop concentrations, the zone engaged by one medium mortar company being not larger than about 7 acres. When the zone contains troops in extensive fortifications, the mortar fire will probably be preceded by artillery firing for destructive effect. Zone fire is conducted at the rate of about 18 rounds per 2 acres per minute. Elevation and deflection is shifted in order to cover a zone adequately, each platoon firing 2 to 4 rounds for every shift of about 50 yards.

Short, intense concentrations are fired at visible targets in exposed positions. These concentrations usually last for 2 to 3 minutes, with the ammunition expenditure being about 50 rounds per 2 acres per concentration.

MASSED MORTAR FIRE

Massing the medium mortars of a regiment to form a provisional medium mortar battalion, is a Red Army practice more likely to be encountered when Soviet troops are on the defensive, or when the situation is relatively stable. Placed under the command of the regimental heavy mortar battery commander, the 27 medium mortars, plus the 6 heavies (120-mm), can fire a barrage 600 to 700 yards wide.

When a provisional mortar battalion organizes its firing position, the companies are echeloned in depth along the front, with intervals of about 100 yards between companies. Dummy and alternate firing positions are prepared, but the battalion usually goes into position rather far forward in order to get the maximum range for its pieces.

When the battalion commander has received the battalion fire mission, he allots separate missions to each of the companies. The battalion sector may be divided among the medium mortar companies for general support purposes. He also designates the reference points, sectors for antipersonnel barrages, accompanying concentrations, and platoon and company phase lines for antitank-antipersonnel barrages, aimed at infantry riding on tanks.

Once the battalion is in position, the pieces are not registered until the order to do so is received from the headquarters of the artillery which is supporting the rifle troops on that particular front. This headquarters designates both the time and duration of the mortar registration. The order in which companies will register their mortars, and the methods of registration, are then set by the battalion commander in order to reduce the registration period, and to avoid interference among the companies.

Within the battalion, communication is by telephone, but for communication with the artillery headquarters and the infantry, radio is used. Once this communication has been established, the battalion commander is able to fire all companies as a single unit. This massing of fire is probably the outstanding feature of Soviet mortar tactics.

When firing a massed antipersonnel barrage, each company is given the coordinates of its right sector line. The pieces are laid so that each company's barrage will fall with the extreme right burst near its sector line. The other bursts then extend to the left across the sector. The command to fire is not given until the enemy infantry has approached to within 200 to 250 yards of the Soviet front-line positions. Then the command to fire is given only on the orders of the infantry commander, or the commander of the artillery group supporting the infantry. If the enemy approaches to within 150 to 200 yards of the front with no orders to fire having been received, then the battalion commander can open fire on his own initiative.

In frontal antipersonnel barrages, fire is conducted in a parallel sheaf fired from fixed settings. Ammunition allotment for such a barrage is 112 rounds per company, and duration of fire is from 2 to 3 minutes. If the enemy attack penetrates the barrage, adjustment is made immediately to reduce the range

100 yards, thus forcing the enemy to advance through another curtain of mortar fire.

SUMMARY

On the whole, Red Army mortar technique is, for the great part, very similar to that of the U.S. Army. The Soviets, however, seem to place greater emphasis on the role of the mortar as a support weapon, and therefore the mortar fire power of a Red Army unit is much greater than its U.S. Army equivalent. The most outstanding feature of the employment of mortars in the Red Army is the standing operating procedure for combining mortar units under one commander and firing the pieces in mass. Although some U.S. units have, on occasion, experimented with this technique, it is not a common practice among our own troops."

22. RUSSIAN ANTITANK TACTICS

Tactical and Technical Trends, No 35, October 7th 1943

While the tank, which has received its greatest exploitation in the present war, has under certain circumstances proved to be a formidable weapon, important successes have been scored against it by artillery and tank-destroyer guns in North Africa.

The tank has, no doubt, accelerated the speed of battle, helped to overcome space, expanded the area of the battlefield, and increased the tempo of attack.

The experience of the Russians on the Eastern Front in combatting large concentrations of German armor can be read with interest and profit. The following article, a translation of Russian reports, deals principally with Russian defensive measures against large-scale German tank attacks in the Orel-Kursk sector.

a. Organization of the Defense

When beginning large offensive operations, the Germans lay the main stress on tanks. They concentrate them on narrow sectors in order to effect a breakthrough and then push through their motorized units and infantry. The problem of the air force and artillery is one of direct support of the tanks on the battlefield. Therefore, defense must be organized so as to repulse the combined blows of the enemy, and especially his tanks. Experience has shown that the best results are gained by the establishment of antitank defense areas.

From reconnaissance data the Russian commander determines the sectors of primary and secondary importance in connection with possible tank attacks. Where the terrain is the more accessible (level or broken, but without deep ravines and swamps) there must be more antitank defense areas. During reconnaissance, the commander determines the most expedient way of using antitank guns and rifles; the location of the sector where they are to be used and the character and type of the most advantageous obstacles under the given conditions. It must be taken into consideration that not all seemingly impassable sectors are actually so. Therefore, it is advisable to organize a system that keeps the approaches to "impassable" tank areas within fire range.

In one case fifteen German tanks attacked the Russian advanced positions. The left flank bordered on a ravine difficult for tanks to pass. The Russian artillerymen easily repulsed three frontal attacks, but the Germans then blew up the steep sides of the ravine and made it passable for tanks. Since the approaches to the ravine were not covered by artillery fire, the enemy tanks broke through and attacked the Russian battery from the rear. It was possible to restore the position only by bringing in the antitank reserve.

The officer directly in command of the antitank defense areas must calculate the amount of fire power and dispositions. The amount of fire power depends upon the density of the tank attack on the given sector. If it happens that there are not enough antitank defenses, the commander requests more from the higher authority. If, however, the commander has only a limited number of antitank guns and rifles, he must not scatter them throughout the defensive positions but must use them on the main sectors.

Certain commanders, in determining the amount of antitank defense calculate on the basis of the theoretical possible density of a tank attack. In reality, however, the Germans have a very limited number of tanks on, many sectors. Therefore, the expected and not the theoretical density of a tank attack must be considered. In case of enemy reinforcements, the antitank defense areas may have to be strengthened.

It is of great importance to have all approaches and intervals between defense areas within range of converging defense fire. In addition, the fire power is disposed so that any tanks, that may have broken into the defense area, may be hit.

b. Disposition of Antitank Guns and Rifles

Combat experience has shown the effectiveness of the following disposition of antitank guns and rifles. Guns are placed at intervals of from 100 to 150 yards and with distances in depth of from 200 to 300 yards. Antitank rifles are arranged in squads. They deliver flank and oblique fire simultaneously with the guns. The intervals between squads of armor-piercing weapons are from 50 to 100 yards and the distances from 100 to 150 yards. With flanking fire, the distance between the guns and rifles must not be over 100 to 150 yards.

c. Cooperation between Defense Areas

Constant communication is maintained between defense areas. There should be complete and detailed agreement as to the methods of cooperation. The distance between the guns on the flanks of the two defense areas should not be over 500 yards. For antitank rifles this distance is reduced to from 150 to 200 yards.

d. Cooperation between Artillery and Infantry Commanders

The artillery commander establishes close contact with the infantry commander of the unit in the region in which the antitank defense is formed. Practice has shown the advantage of sending to the combat outpost a special liaison officer, who, in case of a tank attack, determines the number and direction of action and immediately reports to the defense area.

e. Artillery Tactics Against Tank Attacks

For repulsing large tank attacks, artillery of all calibers and heavy mortars are brought into use. Batteries that fire from concealed positions adjust their fire toward the approaches and antitank obstacles. In case of a tank breakthrough there must be a very detailed agreement with the artillery commanders concerning signals. When conditions dictate, divisional and, at times, heavy artillery may be put out into open fire positions; these should be prepared in advance.

The antitank defense system as a whole is thoroughly camouflaged. Strict discipline in firing must also be observed. It is not necessary to fire from all guns at individual tanks or when they appear in small groups of three to four; it is more advisable to allow them to come within range of direct fire. When the enemy makes mass tank attacks the artillery opens fire at the greatest effective range. In addition, mobile artillery of all calibers and firing from concealed positions is used.

f. Antitank Reserves

Since the antitank defense cannot be equally strong throughout its whole system, antitank reserves are of special importance. The reserves are allocated to threatened sectors by army commanders. It is expedient to prepare in advance firing positions for the reserves on sectors that are more likely to be pierced.

It is well for the next higher headquarters to prepare a plan of maneuver for the antitank reserve. In this plan the composition, commander, line of possible deployment and detailed routes are indicated. It is also well to have a signal (known both to the army commander and the commander of the reserve group) for calling the reserve.

g. An Example of Defense Tactics

German tank attacks in the Orel-Kursk sector were characterized by large concentrated blows of several hundred tanks at a time on narrow sectors of the front. Following the first echelons were the second and third, with the number of tanks increasing each time. There were several instances when the Germans brought over 200 tanks into battle at one time. The air force cleared the way for the tanks, and the tanks in turn cleared the way for the infantry. During the very first days the enemy suffered defeat in the battle for air supremacy. This left the tanks to break through the defense without air support while facing our artillery.

Preceding a concentrated tank attack the enemy conducted combat reconnaissance with small groups of infantry and tanks. This reconnaissance usually began 30 or 40 minutes before the attack. Enemy reconnaissance columns consisted of from 50 to 60 tanks and several self-propelled artillery guns on which infantry men were carried. These detachments were usually supported by 10 to 15 airplanes. As a rule the combat reconnaissance lasted not more than half an hour. In repulsing these groups the minimum of fire power was used in order to keep the main artillery positions concealed.

During the first battles the German tanks at times succeeded in piercing our front line as much as a mile. In one case seven German bombers appeared, escorted by fighters. While these planes began to bomb the front line, another group of bombers coming in to take the place of the first group raided deeper in the rear. Each group was followed by another as they worked their way deeper and deeper into our defense positions. Tanks appeared simultaneously with the third group of bombers. Forty of them deploying along the front and in depth, rushed out at our front line, firing as they came. Several were disabled but a part of them passed the trenches of our first line. Our infantry remained in its positions and exterminated automatic riflemen who were carried on the tanks, blew up two self-propelled guns and burned up one tank as it was crossing the trench.

At this moment Soviet fighters appeared over the battlefield. Several enemy bombers were shot down. The artillerymen made use of this and opened up intensive fire on the tanks but 20 enemy tanks succeeded in penetrating to the depth of half a mile, where they were met by self-propelled cannons. By this time a great air battle was under way and 150 more German tanks came out against our positions.

The lessons learned in the Orel-Kursk sector were that in fighting reconnaissance and first echelon groups it is necessary to: (1) not only repulse tanks but destroy them; (2) do this as quickly as possible since hundreds of tanks follow; (3) solve this problem with the minimum amount of fire in order to keep the disposition of all guns concealed.

The main object of our infantry is to isolate the German infantry from their tanks, annihilate them, and protect our artillerymen from attacks. Our infantry has always remained intact when they do not leave the trenches as enemy tanks cross them. By remaining in the trenches they are able to separate enemy infantry from the tanks and also destroy infantry when it is tank borne.

Battle experience shows that we must strike tanks with concentrated artillery fire and from the air on their initial positions and at the approaches to the battlefield. During the attack it is necessary to allow the tanks to approach to be sure of hitting them. The Orel-Kursk battles show that even tank breakthroughs are not dangerous if the enemy infantry has been separated from the tanks.

23. RUSSIAN EMPLOYMENT OF TANKS

Tactical and Technical Trends, No 18, February 11th 1943

Soviet tactics, like German, are modern in character and show mastery of the entire gamut of weapons in modern war.

The following report deals with various items of information received from the Russian front, and is based mainly on articles which have appeared in the Russian Army newspaper "Red Star." No reference is made specifically to any particular phase of the Russian offensive.

The Russians declare that one of the main lessons of the campaign has been that armored forces alone can never achieve a decisive result; they must receive adequate support from other arms, and particularly from infantry, while they can never hope even to break the crust of a really strong position without the assistance of artillery or heavy bombing. The other arms are essential to deal with enemy artillery, antitank guns, and minefields. Moreover, even if tanks do penetrate a position, when unaccompanied by infantry they can be cut off and successfully dealt with, especially by night. The morale of seasoned troops remains entirely unaffected by the knowledge that isolated tanks are in their rear, for they realize that, provided the enemy infantry can be prevented from joining up with them, the tanks must either retire or be mopped up.

The Russians emphasize that armored vehicles must be concentrated to attack where they can be most effective. If they are supporting infantry they must be put under command of the unit supported, but the temptation to split them up into small groups with the object of helping the infantry forward all along the front must be avoided. Tanks should not be regarded solely as a means of direct attack to overcome strong resistance which is holding up the infantry, but should aim rather at breaking in where resistance is weaker, striking strongly defended localities only in the rear, and ultimately exploiting the "break-in" into a "break-through."

Tank forces in the attack must be accompanied by mobile field and antitank guns, which must be well forward to deal with surprise opposition. They will also be invaluable for repulsing enemy tank counterattack. Russian tank forces rely largely on air support, particularly by dive-bombers, to extend the range of artillery preparation, to harass enemy reserves, and to break up counterattacks.

24. SOVIET TANKS IN CITY FIGHTING

Intelligence Bulletin, May 1946

Special Assault Units Used in Battle for Berlin

In the battle for Berlin, a large city converted by the Germans into a fortress for a last ditch stand, the Russians used massed mechanized units in street battles. However, Soviets do not recommend that tank units be sent into the city, where movement is usually restricted and channelized, barricades and obstacles easily prepared, and every building becomes a potential strongpoint and direct-fire gun emplacement, but the lessons learned during the battle of Berlin are worthy of attention.

Writing in "Red Star," an official Red Army publication, a Major N. Novskov details what was found in Berlin, the difficulties encountered, and some of the methods used to overcome the stubborn German defense.

For the battle of Berlin, the Russians organized combined assault detachments, consisting of one tank battalion, a rifle battalion, a company or platoon of engineers, a battalion of artillery (not less than 122-millimeter), and a platoon of flame throwers.

"Berlin shall remain German!"—that's what the sign on the wall claims, but the crew of this Red Army 122-mm self-propelled gun had something else to say about it. It was with artillery of this type that the Red Army fought into Berlin.

Fundamentally, the defense of Berlin was based on three defensive belts, with intermediate strongpoints: the outer ring of defense along the line of lakes and canals: the ring of defense in the outskirts and suburbs; and an inner ring in the city proper.

The Germans had expected the assault to be made from the East and had concentrated their defenses in that area. Soviet tank units, however, attacked from the south, cutting off the Berlin garrison from the southern German armies which were to have constituted its defense in that sector. The attack in the southern sector moved swiftly, with the Soviets by-passing the main centers of resistance and driving quickly through the outskirts and into the suburbs.

One big obstacle that had to be countered in this first phase was the crossing of the Teltow Canal, where the Germans had demolished all the bridges or had prepared them for demolition. After a thorough reconnaissance, a well organized and coordinated assault was made on the canal and a crossing effected.

In the suburbs, the tanks had a certain degree of maneuverability, due to the larger number of gardens, squares, parks, and athletic fields. They were able to by-pass and envelop separate centers of resistance, to attack some defense fortifications from the rear, and to complete enveloping movements in some cases. Once enveloped, the defense zones in this area quickly collapsed.

In the center of the city, the nature of the fighting was quite different from the fighting in the suburban area. Many-storied buildings in solid masses reduced the maneuverability of tank units. The only avenues of advance were along the streets from building to building. Maneuver was not entirely prohibited, however, for heavily barricaded streets and strongpoints could be enveloped by way of adjacent buildings.

During the battle for the center of the city, the tanks were used

A group of Soviet 152-mm self-propelled gun-howitzers halt on the side of an avenue during the fight for Berlin. The Red Army broke into the German capital by using detachments of tanks, assault guns, infantry, and support troops.

in a supporting role to reinforce the infantry and artillery. The infantry cleared the buildings of antitank gunners who were concealed in the basements or in the lower floors. After the buildings had been cleared, the tanks would advance.

It was in this battle for the center of the city that the combined assault detachments proved their worth. The combined detachment was able to attack with well protected flanks, and could maneuver within the limits of two or three buildings.

The general plan of operations of the assault detachments was as follows: If the detachment met with obstructions, it by-passed the obstruction, or the sappers would blow up the obstacle under the cover of tank and infantry fire. At the same time, the artillery placed fire on the buildings beyond the obstruction, thus blinding the enemy defense and providing additional cover under which the flame throwers set the buildings afire. After demolition of the obstruction, the tanks then rushed forward and tried to get past the enemy defense zone, while the infantry cleared the enemy from the zone itself. Flanks were protected along the side streets by self-propelled mounts or by tanks.

This basic plan was, of course, subject to variation. Depending upon a number of elements, such as the nature of the enemy fortifications, the enemy power of resistance, and the composition of the attacking elements, the tank battalion can attack along two or three streets. Major Novskov asserts that it is better to attack along three streets, keeping the reserve in the center. When the attack is successful along any of the streets, the attacking force is then able to maneuver and envelope the stronger portion of the defensive zone. A tank attack along a larger number of streets leads to a dispersal of force and a reduction in the rate of attack.

Each tank brigade ordinarily had as a main objective the envelopment of from four to six buildings. In the accomplishment of its mission it was found to be of special importance to have a mobile reserve capable of commitment in the direction of the main effort.

Major Novskov states that the boldness of the tankmen played a great role in the street battles. When artificial obstructions were not present, the tanks, with motorized infantry dismounting at high speed, dashed through certain buildings to intersections, squares, or parks, where they took up positions and waited for the infantry. When the infantry had cleared the enemy from the buildings that had been passed by the tanks, the tanks again moved forward in the same manner. When a defended obstacle was encountered, the tank first tried to by-pass it. When it proved to be impossible to by-pass the obstacle, and only when it was impossible, they would begin assault operations.

An example of the action of one assault group is cited by Major Novskov. "While attacking in the direction of the Ringbahn (loop railroad), the tank battalion was stopped in the

Red Army T-34 tanks rendezvous in the rubble of a Berlin square. During combat in the city, Soviet tank battalions, supported by infantry, assault guns, and engineers, attacked on an average front of two to three city streets wide.

northern part of Mecklenburgische Strasse by a reinforced concrete wall 8 meters wide and 2.5 meters high. The barricade was protected by strong machine gun and automatic fire and also by antitank grenade launchers installed in houses at the barricade itself. There were no detours. The commander decided to break through the obstacle. He first sent out a group of submachine gunners whose mission was to annihilate the grenade launchers, which was accomplished in a short period of time. Then 122-millimeter guns opened fire on the houses where the enemy firing points were located. The tanks, advancing simultaneously with the artillery, also opened fire on the buildings on the other side of the barricade. Under cover of the artillery and tank fire assault engineers climbed up to the barricade with explosives. After three explosions in the barricade, a breach was made through which tanks and infantry rushed. The well organized mutual support guaranteed the success of the attack."

In the case of Berlin, used as an example of a large modern city turned into a fortress, the Russians emphasize the importance of mobile reserves; the formation of cooperating teams of tanks, infantry, artillery, and engineers; the importance of heavy artillery ("not less than 122-millimeter"); and the fact that maneuver though restricted by the channelized avenues of advance, can still be performed on a limited scale.

The Soviets further note that the use of massed tanks in the streets of a modern city is not recommended, but that it has been done, and tanks can be used effectively if it is done correctly.

They emphasize the importance of not dispersing the attacking force too greatly, and of attacking on a relatively narrow front for each assault detachment.

25. RED ARMY OFFICERS' CORPS

Intelligence Bulletin, March 1946

Decrees Revive Once-Hated Traditions

The Communist Party and the Soviet Government have recently taken several steps to increase the attractiveness of a postwar career for officers in the Red Army. These innovations, in drastic contrast to the avoidance of special privilege in the Revolutionary period, officially restore the traditional prestige and prerogatives of the Russian officers' corps. The officers' corps, once the symbol of despised Czarist oppression, has been gradually revived until today it is imbued with both old and new Russian fighting tradition, and enjoys a firmly rooted authority based on wartime success and the adulation of the government and the people.

In order to "free officers from personal and economic preoccupations," staff orderlies are now provided for all general officers and colonels, even those on the retired list. The new decree likewise authorizes increased rations of free food and exemptions from war taxes for the officers' corps. Previously, it was announced that separate Red Army officers' clubs were being built in military districts and at garrison posts because "under present conditions of cultural enlightenment it is necessary to have sharp differentiation and separation between officers and enlisted men." Last spring, plans to construct special apartment houses for officers and their families were announced.

These changes are a far cry from the treatment received by officers in the Red Army during the early days of the Soviet Union. During and after the Revolution in the winter of 1917-18, all ranks and grades were abolished, and there existed only two formal and nonpermanent categories—rank and file, and

Although uniform regulations kept officers looking pretty much like enlisted men, prior to the war Red Army officers had already gone far in rank differentiation. These prewar uniforms may be cut like those of enlisted men, but the boots are of good soft leather, the breeches of blue surge, and the tunics of quality OD wool.

commanders. The commanders were distinguished from their men by no insignia other than a small mark on their sleeves (later by a collar tab pip), and the differences between their dress, pay, and treatment were correspondingly small. Socially, all Red Army men were on the same level. This entire program reflected the popular revulsion on the part of both the people and the members of the armed forces against the tradition of oppression

Under the new regulations, officers have really gone to town. This Cossack in field uniform not only wears the re-adopted Czarist-type shoulder boards, but has other traditional gear formerly taboo. Note the beard, the Cossack hat, the Cossack saber and knife. He may wear a Cossack cape and scarf-hood bashlik

Infantry officers in the field still follow an almost world-wide practice of dressing and appearing pretty much like their men. The officer in this group is the lieutenant with the medals (center). He wears a G.I. cap and enlisted man's pocketless tunic; only his shoulder insignia and Sam Browne belt distinguish him.

of the old Czarist officers.

In the first days of the Revolution, officers were subject to deposition and arrest at the hands of soldiers' committees formed in their units. Off-duty saluting and standing at attention were abolished by the First Order of the Petrograd soviet on 14 March 1917. Even the election of officers was seriously discussed, and in order to assure the political reliability of the ex-Czarist commanding personnel, a system of political commissars was instituted in 1917. The political commissars exercised stringent control over commanders during the Civil War. (The commissars alternately lost and regained the power of veto of command decisions until 1942, when they were absorbed into the regular officers' corps.)

So equalitarian was the spirit of the Soviet armed forces that the very word "officer" was abolished from the Soviet vocabulary in 1918 as a hateful reminder of Czarist times. Instead, officers were referred to as company, division, and other unit commanders. External political conditions and the disappearance of pre-revolutionary classes in Russia gradually brought about a change in the position of Red Army officers. During the 1920's unit commanders ate at the same mess as their men and shared the Red Army clubs with them. Pay and living quarters were usually poor.

Revival of the officers' corps was started inauspiciously by the Decree of September 1935, at which time it was believed advisable to revive the prestige of the army and the authority of the commanders. Regulations were passed restoring the familiar designations of the lower grades, reviving the rank of marshal, and granting substantial increases in pay. The decree reestablished individual ranks for commanders. This decree was designed to insure the steady growth of the commanders as a group, to improve their relative standing, to give incentive to greater effort, to reward loyal service, and in particular to reinforce their power and authority. The decree established service as an officer in the Red Army as a lifelong profession, and fixed definite terms of service for the various ranks, providing appropriate distinguishing uniforms and insignia.

The purge of the Red Army in 1937 indicated that the officer class was not considered completely reliable. By 1940, however, the salute became obligatory on all occasions, and the rank of general was reintroduced.

The outbreak of the war with Germany showed the need for insuring the loyalty of the officer class to the government, as well as for increasing the respect and obedience shown to commanders by their men. Determined efforts were made to increase the number of Party members in the rapidly expanding officers' corps. Distinctions of rank were emphasized progressively. The political commissars again lost their veto power in 1942 and officers received many privileges, such as special discounts in state stores; separate stores were established for those of high rank.

The uniforms decreed in 1943 (of which this is service dress) strongly mark the difference between officers and men, and are quite gaudy. The edges of this coat collar and front are piped in the officer's arm color (here red); his dress epaulets have a gold base with red piping. His dress uniform would be even more colorful.

Not until the reintroduction of the pre-revolutionary stiff shoulder boards (pognoy) in January 1943 was a separate classification of commanders revived, along with new and more resplendent uniforms and other accouterments reminiscent of the old days. The Decree of July 1943 finally granted the once-despised title of "officer" to Red Army commanders, and officially and for the first time in Soviet history established a distinct "officers' corps." Other steps were taken to increase the distinction between officers and enlisted men. Differences in pay and treatment rapidly increased, and today the annual pay of a private is 600 rubles, while that of a lieutenant is 7,700 rubles, or almost 13 times as much.

Since the Decree of July 1943 and subsequent measures, the glamour and prestige of the Soviet officers' corps has been confirmed in practice and by decree. The corps is firmly established, conscious of its dignity and special status, and proud of its traditions. As in the American and other armies, the Red Army officers' corps includes large numbers of men recently risen from the ranks and drawn from civil life. The Soviet press, radio, and movies have popularized and glorified the Soviet officer in the minds of the civilian population.

The recent legislation concerning orderlies and officers' clubs has for the most part legalized practices that grew up during the war.

In the early days of the war the recognition granted to officers was primarily designed to strengthen their authority. Now, Soviet policy has the avowed purpose of maintaining a strong army and improving the quality of the officers' corps. In this connection the opening of the Suvorov Schools, primarily for the children of Red Army men killed in battle, was a significant development in 1943. These military schools, which are directly comparable to the Czarist Cadet Schools, will graduate each year approximately 5,000 youths whose education since their 10th year has been largely military. Thus, it should be possible to select the majority of career officer candidates from Suvorov School students.

The army of the U.S.S.R. dates its origin from 1918, but it is deeply proud and aware of the military laurels which have in the past graced Russian arms. Soviet officers are expected to be familiar not only with World War II triumphs but with the campaigns and strategic principles of pre-Soviet heroes. Marshal Stalin told the Red Army on 7 November 1941: "Let the manly images of our great ancestors - Aleksandr Nevski, Dmitri Donskoi, Kuzma Minin, Dmitri Pozharski, Aleksandr Suvorov, Mikhail Kutyzov - inspire you in this war."

26. THE RED ARMY INFANTRYMAN

Intelligence Bulletin, June 1946

The largest ground army of the present day is the Red Army. We may better understand it and its capabilities if we know something about the individual soldier in that army; his origin and civilian training, what he gives and what he gets during his military service, and how and what he is taught in the army.

The Red Army soldier is first of all a Russian. He is the product of the special way of life that exists in the U.S.S.R. as the result of heritage from the past and of present conditions. Some 180 nationalities are included in the U.S.S.R. The Krasnoarmeets (the Red Army soldier) may be any of these nationalities, for every male citizen of the U.S.S.R. is equally

The average Red Army recruit enters military service with a good background of preinduction training. He is also well indoctrinated politically, but as a person he is not unlike many an American G.I.

liable for military service. Under the Universal Military Service law of 1939, all male citizens "regardless of race, nationality, religious belief, educational qualifications, social origin, and position" are subject to military service.

The Soviet Constitution, as well as the Universal Military Service Law, emphasizes the liability of every citizen for military service, for Article 133 states that "the defense of the fatherland is the sacred duty of every citizen of the U.S.S.R."

But from whatever nationality among the Russians he may come, the Red Army recruit goes into the actual military establishment already prepared to carry out his duties as a soldier. He has been a part in a gigantic training program since the first grade of school.

The average Red Army soldier has completed 10 years of

schooling if he is from one of the major cities. If he is from a rural district, he will probably have had at least 7 years of schooling. All during these school years, he has been indoctrinated with the thought that military service is an honor and a patriotic obligation. He has been given military drill, and has had his body built up through exercise all through the first 7 years of school. From the eight through the tenth grades, he has been given preconscription training that is similar to our C.M.T.C. program, but more intensive. The program includes some small-arm range training, 2 weeks of summer military camps, and some company tactics. In short, the Red Army soldier gets a large share of what we call "basic training" before he enters the army.

The recruit is called for his period of military service at the age of 19, or at 18 if he has finished middle school (comparable to our high school) at that age. Certain deferments are granted to those not physically fit and to scientists, rural school teachers, and certain essential workers.

In the army, he serves a period of 2 years. Following the period of active service he goes on an "extended furlough." During that time he may go home and hold a job, but is subject to immediate recall in case of emergency, and is subject to brief training periods. The period of extended furlough lasts from the end of the period of active service, until such time as a total of 5 years of military service is completed.

During his period of active service, the soldier undergoes an intensive program of training. He receives training in weapons and tactics, plus a large amount of subjective training and political indoctrination.

The noncommissioned officer in the Red Army is a product of schools that are similar in purpose and operation to our own regimental NCO schools. Noncommissioned officers must serve a period of 3 years, rather than 2 as do the privates. Most students of the noncommissioned schools are selected from among

The Red Army infantryman travels light. He has a minimum of personal equipment. His uniform is simple and comfortable, consisting primarily of a pullover jacket, baggy trousers, and high-top boots.

volunteers, though some may be detailed to the school. Before World War II, the NCO school lasted for 9 months. During the war, the time was reduced to 3 months. The working day was increased however from 8 hours to 10 to 12 hours.

Officers may come from the ranks or from civil life. In either case, the officer is the product of a series of officer schools. Entrance to the schools is based on educational qualifications or upon the passing of an entrance examination. If successful, the candidate will graduate as a junior lieutenant after 2 years. During the war, the period was reduced to 6 months. Further military education is highly selective and competitive and the officer must show his worth before he is admitted to the higher service schools.

Discipline is strict in the Red Army, though under combat conditions there was not too great a difference made between company-grade officers and enlisted men. A deliberate effort is being made to foster an officer corps, and officers are now receiving many privileges that were not accorded to their predecessors before the beginning of World War II.

The Red Army infantryman travels light. He has a minimum of personal equipment. Tents are seldom used and shelter is improvised from local materials. He has been taught the elimination of nonessentials, and improvisation to meet his needs.

Normally the infantryman is armed with a rifle, carbine, or submachine gun. The water-cooled Maxim is the standard heavy machine gun, while the M1927 Degtyarev is the standard light machine gun used by the infantry squad. Some automatic rifles are carried. All small arms are caliber 7.62 millimeter. While many mortars are used in the Red Army, it is not normally considered an infantry weapon and the mortar crew does not come from the infantry. The Red Army infantrymen's weapons are good, and he has proven that he can use them effectively and well.

Though many an American G.I. will grunt derisively when told that other people walk more than he does, it is true that the Soviet infantryman must depend upon his feet for much of his transportation. There are not as many vehicles assigned to infantryman units in the Red Army as in the U.S., and the majority of those assigned must be used for supply, and as prime movers for artillery and antiaircraft guns, and to haul ammunition.

The Red Army soldier has, like his American counterpart, been granted many benefits as a veteran. During his active service career, however, his pay appears to be a pittance by U.S. standards. The Red Army private receives a total of 600 rubles per year, which is very difficult to access in U.S. dollars, since purchasing power of the ruble to the average Soviet citizen is almost nil. Pay scales range from that of the private to that of a General of the Army, which is 60,000 rubles per year. The equivalent of a private first class receives 1,000 rubles per year; a corporal, 2,000 rubles; a sergeant, 3,000 rubles; a first sergeant, 4,200 rubles. The discrepancy between officer and enlisted pay is great. The first lieutenant receives 12.5 times the pay of a private, or 7,700 rubles per year.

The base pay of Red Army personnel is computed according to the position held, as well as the rank. For instance, a captain's base pay may vary from 8,700 rubles to 9,600 rubles depending upon whether he is an infantry company commander or a mortar company commander. Extra pay is given for long service.

Certain units receive higher pay than others. Guards units, which have distinguished themselves in action, receive double pay in the ranks. There are additional kinds of extra pay for front-line service, up to 100 percent increase over base pay. For instance, in 1942, anti-tank gunners received an increase of 100 percent in their base pay (officers 75 percent) and also got bonuses for each enemy tank destroyed.

Certain extra pay benefits are given those who hold decorations. Decorations also carry with them other benefits, such as free transportation on public conveyances and one round trip ticket per year on the railroads.

As a part of his pay, the soldier receives, in addition, a ration of cigarettes and vodka, movie and theater tickets, and free toilet articles.

The uniform of the Red Army soldier is simple and comfortable. The overhanging shirt, secured at the waist by a wide belt, and the overseas cap with the Red Star emblem are familiar objects to the reader of the daily paper. However, during the war a wide mixture of military and civilian clothing was necessary.

Officers and men wear similar uniforms in the field, but an effort is being made to provide a distinctive officer uniform for garrison and off-duty use.

Both officer and enlisted men wear shoulder boards which

Not all of the Soviet G.I.'s are men. Women, such as the soldier shown here (above, right) have a place among Red Army ground troops. Although most women soldiers are in service and medical units, some have played a combat role.

carry the rank insignia and the color of the branch of service or grade. Olive drab boards are supposed to be worn in the field, but quite often the brighter, dress boards were used. In combat, the Red Army men preferred the overseas cap to the helmet, and the overseas cap was more often worn.

Various special units have their own distinctive insignia and dress. The winter uniform include the well-known parka and white overpants. Fur hats, padded jackets and overcoats are common articles of winter issue.

Guards badges, signifying crack organizations, and wound stripes are worn on the right-hand side of the blouse. Other decorations are worn on the left. The Red Army man wears the medal, rather than the ribbon as do the U.S. troops.

The rations of the Red Army are not elaborate, but are nourishing and heavy. Standard are rich soups and stews of vegetables and meat, garnished with sour cream if possible. One common dish is "kasha," a sort of porridge of buckwheat. In time of war, living off the country is an established practice of the Red Army.

During his entire army career, and before and after, the Red Army man is subjected to instruction in the doctrines and political philosophy of the Communist Party. Many hours of the preconscription training are devoted to political subjects, and during his army career the soldier hears lectures, sees films, and reads literature prepared to educate him in the accepted soviet political thought. In addition, he receives much instruction in the history and traditions of the Red Army. He is also taught to hate the enemy through lectures and films on enemy atrocities. He hears much of heroic acts of the Red Army and of individual Red Army soldiers.

Women play a definite part in the Red Army. Many service troops are women, and much of the cooking of infantry units is done by women. As distinguished from purely the service troops, many women have been used as snipers and in guerrilla fighting. There have been some instances of women being used as combat unit commanders. Red Army nursing personnel quite often operate much closer to the actual fighting than is customary in other armies, and there have been many instances of the nurses accompanying units in combat, much as our battalion aid men do.

This end product of a continuous training cycle, the Red Army soldier, is a hard, determined, courageous individual who is eager to defend Russia. This obligation has been pointed up

Chow in the Red Army is not elaborate, but is nourishing and heavy. Standard are rich soups and stews of vegetables and meat. One common dish is "kasha," a sort of buckwheat porridge.

by the oath that he now takes individually, and not collectively as was the past practice. Usually on Red Army Day, the 1st of May, the Krasnoarmeets, rededicates himself by repeating his enlistment oath.

There are a great number of men prepared to carry out the provisions of that oath. The present strength of the Red Army is near the 6,000,000 mark, and behind the men on active service are large numbers of reservists, many of whom are combat veterans of World War II.

More from the same series

Most books from the 'Eastern Front from Primary Sources' series are edited and endorsed by Emmy Award winning film maker and military historian Bob Carruthers, producer of Discovery Channel's Line of Fire and Weapons of War and BBC's Both Sides of the Line. Long experience and strong editorial control gives the military history enthusiast the ability to buy with confidence.

The series advisor is David McWhinnie, producer of the acclaimed Battlefield series for Discovery Channel. David and Bob have co-produced books and films with a wide variety of the UK's leading historians including Professor John Erickson and Dr David Chandler. Where possible the books draw on rare primary sources to give the military enthusiast new insights into a fascinating subject.

| Barbarossa |  Eastern Front: Encirclement | Götterdämmerung |  Eastern Front: Night Combat |

| The Waffen SS in the East 1941-1943 |  The Waffen SS in the East 1943-1945 | The Wehrmacht Experience in Russia |  Winter Warfare |

| The Red Army in Combat | Wehrmacht Combat Reports: The Russian Front |

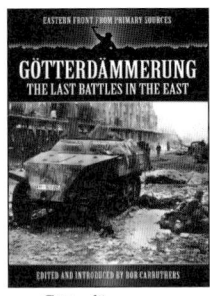

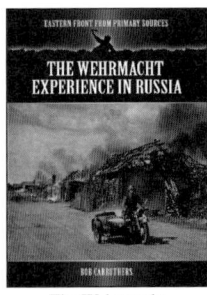

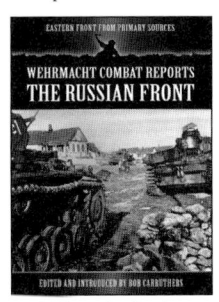

For more information visit www.pen-and-sword.co.uk